The

EQUAL OPPORTUNITIES HANDBOOK

How to deal with everyday issues of unfairness

Third Edition

PHIL CLEMENTS AND TONY SPINKS

KOGAN PAGE

First published as *The Equal Opportunities Guide*, 1994
Second edition, 1996
Third edition, entitled *The Equal Opportunities Handbook*, 2000

Kogan Page Limited
120 Pentonville Road
London N1 9JN

British Library Cataloguing in Publication Data

A CIP record for this book is available from the British Library

ISBN 0 7494 3119 9

Typeset by JS Typesetting, Wellingborough, Northants
Printed and bound in Great Britain by Bell & Bain Ltd, Glasgow

Contents

Acknowledgements

Many people have helped shape my ways of seeing EO over the years. Some have either directly or indirectly assisted with this third edition. Victoria Kern helped with the original graphics. Richard Griggs and all my research 'victims' gave me different perspectives. Robin Oakley and Diana Yach both had major influence on me, and lately, Tim Meaklim and Keith Wood have asked penetrating questions. In my co-author Tony, I have a friend and colleague whose opinions I respect and value. Most of all I have constant constructive critics in Heather, Tom and Matthew without whose unstinting support I would never have the opportunity to complete projects like this.
  PC

Over the years that I have been training and writing on the subject of equal opportunities and fair treatment; I have talked with, learned from and been influenced by many good people including Laurie Trott, Richard Griggs, Guy Hewlett, Ralph Withers, Raoul Dero, Shafiq Mogul, James Kilty, Robin Oakley and Lynne Segal. Too numerous to mention are the many students I have facilitated who, in their own ways, have tested my own commitment to and thinking on this subject. Richest of all these collaborations has been my work, both practical and written, with my co-author Phil Clements whose knowledge and skill continue to inspire me. As with other large ventures I have benefited from the love and support of my wife Jane throughout this project.
  TS

Introduction

In our society there are people, just like you and me, who every day are having to face prejudice and discrimination merely because they happen to be different in some way from the majority. It may be the colour of their skin, their religious beliefs, because they are a woman, because they have a disability, or because they are gay or lesbian. Getting rid of such unfairness and inequality is what equal opportunities is all about.

WHO IS THIS BOOK FOR?

Books are typically aimed at target audiences and written specifically for them. In *The Equal Opportunities Handbook* we have tried to present the issues in a clear and readable way which will be of value to a very wide audience. Employee, student, manager, teacher, nurse, civil servant, trainer, man or woman in the street – we all need to know the issues. Whoever you are, without an understanding of how prejudice and discrimination arise and operate, you are unlikely to be able to eliminate them from your own behaviour. By raising your awareness and increasing your knowledge in this area you will be better able to treat people with fairness and sensitivity.

If you are a trainer, in addition to being able to brush up your own knowledge of the issues, you will be able to use the book as a valuable text in equal opportunities issues for your students either before a course, or as a text to reinforce the issues afterwards.

If you are an employer you will be able to use the book to provide your staff with a ready reference to the main issues of equality, and in doing so help to give meaning and bite to equal opportunities policies. You may bear legal responsibility for the actions of your staff (you may have heard this called 'vicarious liability'), and this may include the payment of compensation to the victim, should your company be found liable. Your staff need to know: this book will help.

As an employer you will also need to think carefully about the issue of institutional discrimination, considering whether the ways you do business are fair to all. Because this area of equal opportunities is of increasing importance we have dedicated a separate chapter to it which will help guide you in your efforts to avoid discriminatory or prejudicial practices.

If you are an employee, there are many areas where you MUST treat people equally because if you don't, among other things:

- you may not get or keep your job;
- you may not get promoted;
- you may fall foul of the law;
- you may lose money if your pay is linked to performance.

At your workplace you have a personal responsibility to be fair to your colleagues and customers (in the broadest sense of the word) and may be held liable for actions which are considered discriminatory. In larger organizations there is likely to be an equal opportunities policy with which you have to comply.

You may simply be a person who wants to know more about the issues, have been a victim of inequality of some kind, or be involved in a real-world equal opportunities problem.

WHY HAVE A HANDBOOK ON EQUAL OPPORTUNITIES?

We believe that the whole subject of equal opportunities is surrounded with mystique, and one of the things that may put you off this subject is a belief that you need expert knowledge in each of the areas of equal opportunities, in order to avoid prejudice and discrimination. We believe that this is not the case. By adopting skills which fit all types of situation, you will be able to think about, and behave towards everyone – regardless of their colour, gender, sexuality, disability or religion – with fairness, courtesy and sensitivity.

We hope this book will:

- help you check your own behaviour and attitudes for fairness, and offer hints and guidance that is practical, realistic and usable in the real world;
- introduce you, in straightforward language, to the most important issues in equal opportunities and fair treatment;
- give you information about racism, sexism, disability, sexuality, and religion, which will help you to be more sensitive and behave more fairly;
- raise your awareness of your own views in these important areas, by asking you questions;
- provide you with some 'fair treatment' skills which apply to a variety of situations;
- explode some of the more common equal opportunities myths; and
- offer you hints, advice and guidance on issues such as language, helping others, and avoiding discriminating behaviour yourself.

HOW TO USE THE BOOK

A glance through the contents page will give you a flavour of what is covered. Most of the chapters stand alone, allowing you to dip into the issues which concern you most, or to look up the specific information you need. The 'issues' chapters begin with a set of objectives which will help you get an idea of where your reading and thinking will be taking you.

We have used side-headings to help you find your way around the text more easily. They will be particularly useful where the book is used in training settings, or where you need to refer back to a particular point. From time to time we challenge you to think more specifically. You will find 'pause for thought' sections scattered throughout the book. Try to make use of these, because they are designed to help you get the most from your reading.

There will always be a question mark over who has the right to publish a book on equal opportunities. Can men justifiably write on the subject of sexism, white people on the subject of racism, able-bodied people on disability and so on? As trainers in this field for many years we have spoken to and worked with people on both sides of prejudice and discrimination. It is out of that experience that we offer you this book; not as the complete solution, but as a helpful guide aimed at ordinary people who have a genuine desire to think and behave fairly.

PERSONAL ACTION PLANS

Equal opportunities is unlike many other subjects in that it will touch almost every aspect of your own daily life, both in terms of the way you interact with others and the way they interact with you. Throughout the book we present issues that you are invited not only to consider on an intellectual level, but also to respond to in some way. If you find this process difficult or challenging, then it is very likely that you are coming to see the world in a new or different way. To help you think through your own response to certain issues, we have included a personal action plan at the end of the relevant chapters.

Chapter 1

How to be Fair

In this opening chapter we will suggest that equal opportunities and fair treatment need not be the complicated minefield that many believe it to be. By exploring the nature of prejudice and its common roots we show how you can equip yourself with a sound understanding of the ways in which prejudice can and does arise, and in so doing offer ways in which it might be addressed. We also explain a system of transferable skills which will enable you to think about and behave towards others with fairness and sensitivity. Having read this chapter we hope you will have a better understanding of:

- what prejudice, stereotyping, labelling and discrimination mean;
- the importance of reflective thinking;
- some of the root causes of prejudice; and
- some transferable skills that will help you treat people fairly.

INTRODUCTION

One of the things that sets the subject of equal opportunities apart from other subjects is that it has become surrounded by worrying myths and seems something of a minefield for the unwary.

equal opportunities is often seen as a minefield

We have met and spoken with many people who share a common apprehension about equal opportunities: they *want* to be fair and treat people equally but are worried that they might easily say or do the wrong thing and upset or offend somebody.

Additionally, there are others who believe, or have been told, that equal opportunities and fair treatment is a hugely complicated subject, needing expert knowledge about each of the various different minority groups they may come into contact with.

fair behaviour and thinking fits most situations

We hope to show you that whilst it is helpful to know about the cultures and concerns of specific minority groups (knowledge that this book will certainly seek to give you) it is not essential. Instead, we will argue that by equipping yourself with certain *transferable* skills and *general* ways of thinking and behaving, you will still be able to extend fair treatment to all individuals and groups whether or not you have specific knowledge of them.

PREJUDICE

At the centre of many of the things we will be speaking about in this book, whether racism, sexism or discrimination against members of the disabled or the gay community, lies the issue of prejudice. Unfortunately, for such an important and central issue, there is a great deal of confusion and argument as to what may or may not amount to prejudice.

In our view these various arguments are largely academic and serve only to obscure thinking about how to overcome prejudice in whatever form it may arise. It is very easy to hide behind such debate, arguing that the way you think about or behave towards certain people cannot possibly amount to prejudice for this reason or that.

What is important is that you should think about your own attitudes and behaviour and the effects they might have on others. For example, are there times when you tend to make assumptions about what people are like, prejudging them even though you haven't met them and know little about them from direct personal experience?

Identifying prejudice through reflective thinking

One of the main themes of this book is what we call 'reflective thinking'. What we mean by this is the ability to reflect back on our attitudes and behaviour and to think through our experiences honestly. The old saying 'we should try to learn from our mistakes' is an appropriate one here, but before any of us can learn from mistakes we must first *accept* that a mistake has been made, and then *reflect* on what needs to be done to avoid making the mistake in the future.

use reflective thinking

We need to push our tendency to justify and defend our views and behaviour to one side, in favour of some honest reflection on the way we actually think about and behave towards others, particularly those who are different from us in some way.

A good time to use reflective thinking is when there has been some form of conflict or argument, or when we feel angry towards a person or group of people. It's easy and natural simply to blame the other person, isn't it? We have all done it, and by blaming the other person we ensure that we remain safe and comfortable. The trouble with this approach is that it increases the chances of further conflict or resentment in the future, whether with the same person or others. Instead, why not try a bit of reflective thinking by following this sequence:

reflection is particularly useful after conflict

- If you feel angry or 'wound-up', allow yourself to calm down.
- Make an agreement with yourself that you are going to reflect on what's taken place. Be honest and, if necessary, critical of yourself (not easy!).
- Go through what has happened in your own mind.
- Don't lay blame, but instead try to capture how things happened.

- Ask yourself why you acted or reacted in certain ways.
- Ask yourself why the other person(s) acted or reacted in the ways that they did.
- Try to identify how *you* contributed to their behaviour.
- Ask yourself what it was about the other person that upset or angered you: was it who they were, how they looked, how they behaved, or a combination of all of these things?
- Could you have acted differently, and if you had acted differently would it have changed the incident for the better?

We have mentioned reflective thinking in some detail because it is such a powerful tool in overcoming prejudice. All too often our own prejudices remain hidden from ourselves, covered up with layers of justification and rationalization that we have created over the years.

Exposing such prejudices is uncomfortable (that's why we keep them buried in the first place). Unfortunately, even though we may think they are under control, bolted down so that they won't affect our behaviour towards others, the truth is they can and often do. The best way to avoid this happening is to identify our prejudices and to confront them head-on, and the best way to do that is by adopting reflective thinking.

identify and confront prejudice

DEFINITIONS OF PREJUDICE

You might say, 'it's all very well you saying that I should try and identify my prejudices in order to confront and start dealing with them, but I still don't fully understand what prejudice is!'

The point is we cannot supply you with a universal definition of prejudice, like a ruler with which to measure your attitudes and behaviour. You need to develop a clear idea of the way that you think about and behave towards other people who are different from you and to question in your own mind whether such views and behaviour are justifiable and fair.

Having said that, there are things that we *can* explain which might help you in this process. Implicit in the word prejudice is the idea of prejudgement, of making your mind up about something before you have any personal experience of or facts about it. Therefore prejudice against a certain group, black people for example, suggests prejudging members of that community before you know anything about them or have had any shared experiences with them.

prejudice is about prejudgement

Pause for thought

- Try to identify a time when, on reflection, you made up your mind about a person or group of people before you had even met them. Perhaps you decided what they were like based on what someone else had told you about them. What effect did that have on your subsequent experience of the person or group?

Stereotyping and prejudice

It might not always be the case that you have absolutely no knowledge or experience of a particular person or group of people. You may know bits and pieces about them or may have even met one or two. However, prejudice often involves a process of filling in the gaps in your knowledge or experience, and this is where stereotyping comes in.

This is another word which has confused and frustrated people looking at the area of fair treatment and equal opportunities, it can often be a trigger for turning people off. Put simply, stereotyping is where you believe that just because people are members of a particular visible group, they must (because of that fact) also share particular traits which you think are characteristic of that group. The reasons you may believe that they share those traits may be because this is what you have been told, or maybe it is what you have experienced.

prejudice and stereotyping are linked

For example, if the first time you meet a disabled person he/she is a wheelchair user who appears heavily dependent upon the assistance of others, you may form the view that such dependence is a common characteristic shared by other members of the disabled community, even though you have no direct experience or knowledge that this is in fact the case.

Myth

'People always talk about prejudice as if it is a negative thing. You can have positive prejudices too, you know!'

Myth-buster

Whilst this may be true, the fact remains that in the area of equal opportunities and fair treatment the *real and pressing* issue is the negative side of prejudice. Negative prejudgement serves to pigeon-hole members of a particular community by sticking various negative labels on them. The argument about positive prejudice merely deflects attention away from the very real problems of negative prejudice.

Labelling

One very real danger arising out of both prejudice and stereotyping is that it is all too easy to label people. Think about yourself for a moment. You rightly expect others to treat you as an individual in your own right, to get to know you before they make judgements about the type of person you are. Prejudice and stereotyping don't allow for this; instead the other person is labelled as having certain characteristics – weakness, laziness, lack of honesty and so on – and these labels then obscure all other thinking about the person. It's not difficult to imagine how frustrating and unfair this must feel, even more so when it happens at interviews, appraisals or in other circumstances where life opportunities are at stake.

Attributes and characteristics

One of the things that is rarely explained in discussions on equal opportunities is that the basis for prejudice, the fact that a person is different from us in some way, is often based upon attributes or characteristics that the person him/herself cannot change. People cannot change their skin colour, their gender, their disability, their accent, etc. This is a crucial point, because what *can* be changed is the prejudice itself and the attitudes and behaviour that result.

Bolting down attitudes

In the years that we have been involved in equal opportunities training one particular argument seems to occur with great regularity, an argument that is extremely relevant to our discussion of prejudice and stereotyping. The argument goes something like this:

- You say that prejudice shows itself through people's attitudes and their behaviour and you make it sound as though my attitudes are linked to my behaviour in such a way that attitudes influence and even drive behaviour.
- I disagree with that argument. I can quite easily think what I like about certain types of people as long as I don't let it show when I have to deal with them.

can we really
bolt down our
attitudes?

Often people who voice this argument describe a situation where they feel able to 'bolt down' prejudices, as if they have secured a big steel door over the place in their subconscious where these thoughts and feelings are kept. Happy that their prejudices are safely locked away and bolted down they then feel comfortable in the belief that they can then deal with others fairly, without such prejudices influencing their behaviour.

This belief is completely misguided. Our behaviour is so closely linked to our underlying attitudes, opinions and beliefs that they show through both verbally and, more importantly, non-verbally (in what is sometimes called body language), especially when we feel under pressure. The stress and anxiety caused in situations of disagreement, conflict or when we find our integrity challenged, weaken and loosen the bolts on that door and our prejudices, no longer containable, leak out.

Discrimination

Another word often used alongside prejudice is discrimination. We will be exploring discrimination in more detail in other parts of this book but it would be useful here to consider how discrimination might contrast with prejudice and how, in fact, it grows out of it.

Whereas prejudice is about the ideas we hold of others who are different from us and about the negative assumptions and prejudgements we might make about them, discrimination is about the way we act. When we act more favourably towards one group of people than another and that favouritism is based on prejudice, then we may be said to have discriminated.

For example, where a person who is black fails to get promotion because her boss holds prejudiced views about black people, a discriminatory act has occurred. The boss has acted upon his prejudice and has dealt less favourably towards the person as a result. We will see in Chapter 10 that such discrimination is against the law.

discrimination is prejudice in action

COMMON THEMES IN PREJUDICE AND DISCRIMINATION

In the introduction we suggested that many people anticipate that equal opportunities and fair treatment will be a hugely complicated subject, requiring specific skills and expert knowledge in respect of each minority group and each form of prejudice and discrimination. One of the reasons this is not so is that prejudice itself, no matter whom it is directed against, has its roots in certain common factors.

Whether racism or sexism, prejudice directed against the disabled community or the elderly, the gay community or the young, each form has common roots (see Figure 1.1). By exposing and understanding these roots, prejudice and the resulting discrimination become more understandable and easier to address.

We believe that the main roots of prejudice are:

- ignorance;
- power;
- vulnerability;
- upbringing; and
- conformity.

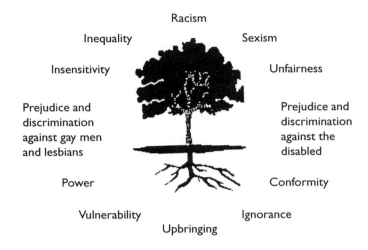

Racism

Inequality   Sexism

Insensitivity   Unfairness

Prejudice and   Prejudice and
discrimination   discrimination
against gay men   against the
and lesbians   disabled

Power   Conformity

Vulnerability   Ignorance
Upbringing

Figure 1.1   *Prejudice and discrimination in all its forms has its roots in things we can often, if not always, change, provided we are aware of them*

Ignorance

We have already said that an important part of both prejudice and stereotyping is a lack of direct knowledge and experience of another person who is different from us. Not knowing why people do certain things, follow certain cultural traditions, speak and dress in certain ways and act differently, we are inclined to provide our own explanations and interpretations and to fill in the gaps in our knowledge and experience by using stereotyped labels. In ignorance, we often interpret such differences as a threat and the explanations that we build, again in ignorance, tend to be heavily negative as a result.

The flip-side to this argument is that the more we know about and understand another person or group of people who are different from us, the less we will find their behaviour and views strange and threatening. If we obtain an accurate explanation of why they do what they do, we will no longer need to invent our own or to fill in the gaps in our previously sketchy knowledge. It follows that one effective way to overcome prejudice is by overcoming ignorance. This book aims to help in this regard by providing you with information in an easy-to-read style that will help to increase your knowledge and understanding of various minority groups and communities.

not knowing can lead to feeling threatened

Pause for thought

• Where are the gaps in your knowledge of other groups?
• What could you do to fill them?

Power

Prejudice is also rooted in power. The power of being in the majority group, for example, can strengthen the belief that people who are in some way outside this group pose a threat to it. In some ways the majority depend upon the existence of minority groups, as it is by setting themselves apart from members of those minority groups that they are able to feel secure in their identity and group membership.

majority group power is threatened by minorities

Power has a lot to do with an aspect of prejudice and discrimination that is termed 'institutional', in that it is a form of prejudice contained within the social system and within institutions such as education, health, government etc which make that social system up, we will be saying more about this aspect of prejudice and discrimination elsewhere in the book.

As an individual reading this book you might well question the relevance of power to a consideration of your own prejudices. But it is important to remember the ways in which you can or do exercise power over others. This may be in your capacity at work, or as a member of a community group or a trades union, responsible for decision making or policy review.

Pause for thought

• Are you in a position to wield 'institutional power'?
• What checks and balances are there on your power?

Vulnerability

An important part of any understanding of prejudice requires that we ask the question 'why should the fact that someone is different from us lead to a negative prejudgement of who and what they are?' We have already discussed the parts that ignorance and power play in this and we have mentioned the idea that difference comes to be interpreted as threatening.

Some reactions to immigration give voice to these fears . . . 'they'll swamp us', 'they'll dilute our culture'. Taking sexism as another example, we hear arguments like 'women shouldn't take men's jobs when there's so much unemployment'. Prejudging people and their cultures and abilities is one way in which we try to cope with our feeling of vulnerability – the vulnera-

prejudice is a way of avoiding feeling vulnerable

bility of our way of life, vulnerability regarding the allocation of jobs, in fact anything we feel we need to cling to for our security.

Another important point to be made here is that such feelings of vulnerability can arise when we think that others may threaten our current view of the world by putting forward alternative ideas and explanations of how things are or should be. For example, a part of the prejudice displayed toward gay men and women arises from the fear that their lifestyle and sexual orientation threatens the view of right and wrong held by the majority. But by recognizing vulnerabilities and how prejudice can spring from them, we are already in the business of addressing our prejudices and of identifying them in others.

Pause for thought

- Review the things you value highly, believe strongly or have strong attitudes towards.
- How did they arise?

Upbringing

When you take time to do some reflective thinking about your own attitudes and opinions in this area, ask yourself whether the way you think and the values and attitudes you hold differ from those of your parents and close friends. We all like to think of ourselves as free-thinking individuals with minds of our own, but often we don't fully realize and appreciate the impact of our upbringing.

Of course it may be that the influence your parents and close friends have had on your own thinking is largely positive, and if this is the case, that's great! On the other hand, you may decide that values and attitudes you now wish to question, and which you suspect may give rise to certain prejudices, can be traced to your upbringing.

try examining your own attitudes, beliefs and values

We would encourage you, if you feel up to it, to examine your beliefs, attitudes and values regarding others who are different from you. This is in no way an easy or comfortable thing to do, as it requires that you dig underneath layers of defence and justification built up over the years. You will find, as we did, that you have convincing arguments as to why you hold certain views and think in certain ways.

Try, however, to examine your values, attitudes and beliefs from the viewpoint of the other person. If you are white, imagine instead that you are a member of the black community who has come along to listen to and judge these (your) views and opinions about black people. Or imagine that you are a member of the disabled community, considering just how valid this other person's views (yours, of course) on disabled people are.

Conformity

No one likes being out on a limb, isolated because they have disagreed with the views of the majority. Often our need to be liked and to fit in is far stronger than our resolve to stand up against attitudes and behaviour of others which we don't like and don't agree with.

Instead, most of us, for most of the time, simply conform, going along with others even when we know we should really oppose them. Of course, when it comes to equal opportunities and fair treatment, this becomes even more of a live and challenging issue. When others are openly racist or sexist or show open hostility or hatred towards members of minority groups, the chances are, whilst you may not like or agree with it, you'll say nothing.

conformity is easy – challenging is not!

However, by doing so you become involved in such behaviour through your inactivity and some would say that by doing nothing you become as guilty as the person exhibiting the behaviour. While this is a harsh and challenging viewpoint, it is difficult to deny. But by recognizing how conforming may amount to prejudice, you have raised your awareness of another way in which prejudice may be addressed.

Pause for thought

● Take a few moments to think about an example of prejudiced behaviour you have witnessed or heard about. Can you identify any form of vulnerability given voice by the person's behaviour?
• Taking the same or another example of prejudiced behaviour, can you identify aspects of ignorance or power in it?
• How would you challenge such behaviour?

TRANSFERABLE SKILLS

In the final part of this chapter we will discuss a number of transferable skills that will reinforce the message that, far from being a complicated minefield full of traps and pitfalls, equal opportunities and fair treatment are, in fact, simply an extension of skills that you already have and know how to use.

In fact you already make use of most of these skills in your day-to-day dealings with other people. With a little refinement and thought you will see that they are equally applicable to equal opportunities and fair treatment issues.

Before we turn to these skills, however, it is worth hammering home a point that will crop up throughout this book. Treating others fairly, sensitively and with courtesy should not and must not become marginalized as 'equal opportunities' simply because it is applied to a member of a minority

equal opportunities is about daily interaction with other people

group. If I am a member of the gay community I don't want to think that the person I am speaking to is being courteous only because he/she is indulging in a bit of equal ops – I want to feel that they are doing it because I am a person, just like they are, who deserves such common courtesy.

The six main skills

Although there may well be others, we shall concentrate here on six main transferable skills (see Figure 1.2) that you can use to overcome prejudice and discrimination. These are:

- empathy;
- understanding;
- raised awareness;
- sensitivity;
- consequences; and
- a desire to be fair.

Empathy

Too often, people confuse empathy with sympathy, so it is well worth attempting a basic definition of empathy for the purposes of this section. By empathy we mean putting yourself in the other's position and imagining how they might think and feel in the circumstances. The well-known saying 'put yourself in the other person's shoes' is a good starting point for getting to grips with the idea of empathy, but we need to take the idea slightly further than this. We would encourage you not only to place yourself in the other person's position but to look back at yourself and your own behaviour from their position.

Take as an example a situation in which, if you are a white person, you are about to tell a racist joke. Before telling the joke imagine how it would feel if you were a black person overhearing it (this is putting yourself in the other's position). How would you feel to be on the receiving end of this type of humour? Would you still think it was humorous? Now, still imagining yourself in the other person's position, imagine how you must appear to them. You would probably seem to be someone who is at best insensitive, and at worst racist. Using empathy, you should be able to think about and reflect upon your behaviour, thinking through its consequences. This is a good test when you are unsure whether your behaviour might offend others.

Understanding

Linked closely with the ability to use empathy is the need to develop your understanding in various areas, including:

having empathy is not the same as having sympathy

understand your attitudes and behaviour

- the ways in which your attitudes may amount to prejudice, as we discussed in the earlier part of this chapter;
- the ways in which your attitudes can affect your behaviour and thus potentially lead to discriminatory or prejudiced behaviour;
- the types of behaviour that might lead to a lack of fairness or reveal prejudice;
- the consequences of your attitudes and behaviour for yourself and for others; and
- the need to utilize empathy and sensitivity in order to avoid offending others.

. . . and their consequences

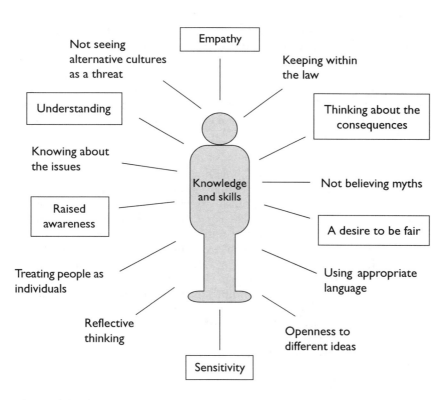

Figure 1.2 *Some of the knowledge, skills and attitudes which are able to fit into almost any situation, so that you can think and behave fairly, regardless of who the individual or group happens to be. The six main skills are shown in boxes*

Raised awareness

We would also encourage you to become far more aware of the effects your behaviour has or may have on others and of their reactions to that behaviour. Adopting an attitude that boldly states 'Well, people must take me as they find me' is bound to lead to friction and conflict sooner or later.

develop an
awareness of
the needs of
others

You should also try to develop a raised awareness of any special courtesies or needs that the other person may have. As an example, imagine that you are chatting with a person who is deaf but is nonetheless an accomplished lip-reader. By using empathy and a little understanding of the situation you will realize that to assist the lip-reader you should keep your hands away from your mouth when talking. You shouldn't look away in mid-sentence, and there is no need to exaggerate your lip movements or to shout (as some people are inclined to do when speaking with a person who is deaf or has hearing difficulties).

Remember that raised awareness, as with the other skills in this section, is a *transferable skill* that will stand you in good stead no matter whom you are dealing with or talking with.

Another very good way of raising your awareness is thinking about your use of language. Think about what you are saying and how you say it, as these are the messages that others will pick up whether they are your intentional audience or are nearby and overhear your remarks! This is dealt with further in Chapter 2.

Sensitivity

sensitive is not
soft

By raising your awareness of the things mentioned here and elsewhere in the book, you will increase your sensitivity to both people and situations – an important and transferable skill. For men the word often conjures up images of being soft and of losing some of that macho masculinity. We believe, however, that if macho means being insensitive or hard, then being macho is simply bad news. Wake up guys! No one loses face for being sensitive to the opinions, thoughts and feelings of others.

We expect others to pick up on how we are feeling and not to stamp all over our feelings and opinions, and in turn they expect the same from us. This is what sensitivity is all about, particularly when you are in situations with people who have different ways of thinking and perhaps behaving, different cultural backgrounds and values or different needs.

Consequences

Pretty much everything we do, especially when it is directed at someone else, has consequences. This is particularly true of equal opportunities and fair treatment issues, where behaviour which may be racist or sexist, or which may lack sensitivity, understanding or reveals prejudice, may have quite serious consequences for all parties concerned.

Thinking through the likely consequences of your actions is a great way of working out whether you're on the right track. It could stop you making a prejudiced decision or inadvertently putting your foot in it and offending someone. On the other hand it might push you into taking action in a situation where keeping quiet would make you as bad as the person displaying the prejudiced behaviour.

always ask 'what are the likely consequences?'

Pause for thought

- Refer back to the exercise on reflective thinking. How does considering the consequences of your actions fit in with reflective thinking?

A desire to be fair

You cannot play at fair treatment, seeking to put it on like a new coat when the situation demands and take it off and hang it on the peg when the need has passed. The things we have spoken about in this chapter require that you have a genuine desire to reflect upon and, where necessary, change your existing attitudes and behaviour in order to address your prejudices, allowing you to behave in a fair, non-prejudicial and non-discriminatory way towards others who are different from you.

a lack of sincerity is usually easily spotted

People are usually much better than *you* might anticipate at spotting a lack of genuineness or identifying a person merely playing the game or paying lip-service to these issues. In our experience, a consistent reason for equal opportunities policies in a variety of settings failing to have real impact is that those charged with implementing them only do so half-heartedly. We hope that, as you are reading our book, the likelihood is that you *do* have a genuine desire to be fair and wish to learn ways of doing that.

KEY POINTS IN THIS CHAPTER

- Prejudice involves making judgements about other people or other groups before you have any direct knowledge or experience of them. We are concerned in this book with *negative* prejudice.
- Stereotyping, which is part and parcel of prejudice, involves a belief that all the members of a particular group share certain, usually negative, traits or characteristics.
- Discrimination is when you act on such prejudices by dealing with particular people less favourably than others for no good reason.
- Most prejudice is based on the things in others which make them different from the majority. These are usually things which the person or group cannot change, e.g. skin colour.

- All types of prejudice have common roots. These include ignorance, power, vulnerability, the influence of upbringing, and conformity. By using reflective thinking, you can unearth these root causes and be better placed to address them for yourself.
- By developing a set of transferable skills – reflective thinking, empathy, understanding, raised awareness, sensitivity, an understanding of consequences and a desire to be fair – you will have the tools you need to extend equal opportunities.

PERSONAL ACTION PLAN

Try answering the following questions:

How will the things I have learnt in this chapter change the way I think and act towards others who are different to me?

What has this chapter helped me to learn about myself with regard to:

- my beliefs;
- my attitudes;
- my values;
- my knowledge of others;
- my behaviour;
- my use of language;
- my responsibilities;
- the way I see the world?

How do I need to change in order to become:

- fairer;
- more sensitive;
- more understanding;
- less prejudicial;
- less discriminatory;
- better able to deal with people according to their needs?

If I were to change one thing about the way I act as a result of reading this chapter what would it be?

Chapter 2

The Role of Language

Language has a *vital* role to play in treating people fairly. After you have read this chapter through you should have a good idea of the following:

- why language is so important;
- two general guidelines to follow;
- language and humour;
- language and labelling;
- exclusionary language; and
- problems associated with specific words and phrases.

THE IMPORTANCE OF LANGUAGE

What's in a word?

The fact that you are reading this book suggests that you are at least thinking about issues of equal opportunity. It may be that you are just wondering what all the fuss is about, or you may want to be that little bit better informed so that you can, as far as possible, treat people fairly. You probably won't agree with everything which follows, but at least we hope to present you with some issues which will convince you that language has a very powerful influence in equal opportunities.

what is all the fuss about?

Just talking about the issues will lead you into using some of the terminology of equal opportunities. This chapter is designed to explain some of the terms in current use and establish whether they are always appropriate. It concludes with a selection of words and phrases which, if we are serious about treating people fairly, need careful consideration as to their use.

Pause for thought

Do you use language which may:

- exclude individuals or groups?
- stereotype?
- suggest you may have prejudged people or groups in negative terms?

First of all, here are two general guidelines to follow.

GUIDELINES FOR USING LANGUAGE WHICH IS FAIR

There are two fundamental principles in making sure that your language is fair. It should be *sensitive* and *appropriate*. Both of these are, of course, very subjective. One person's view of what is sensitive and appropriate may be very different from another's, but that's no reason to avoid trying. Let's deal with each of them in turn.

language should be sensitive and appropriate

Sensitivity

How often do we stop to think about the effect our words are having on other people? At school, we may have come across the rhyme 'sticks and stones may break my bones but names will never hurt me'. Whilst we may have tried to cling on to the truth of that rhyme for comfort when other children *were* calling us names, I wonder if it was really true? The fact of the matter is that names *do* hurt, and words can wound the emotions just as painfully as a knife might slide between the ribs.

names do hurt

The point of this is that the insensitive use of words can be a very effective method of discrimination against others, whether intentionally or unintentionally used in that way. Words are particularly powerful because they can be subtle and low level, persistent but not necessarily obvious. Seemingly innocent words can be given a prejudiced ring just by changing the emphasis. The word Arab, for example, is straightforward enough, but put the stress on the A and get A-rab and the speaker very probably means the word to have a derogatory meaning.

words can be an effective method of discrimination

We need to say a few words about sensitivity. You will no doubt be able to think of language which is totally *insensitive* and examples of language which is entirely the opposite, taking full account of the needs and feelings of the people to, or about, whom it is used.

Figure 2.1 shows the two ends of a scale of sensitivity. We would probably place outright racist language or outright sexist language at the left-hand extreme. By the same token, language which is careful and caring would be at the opposite end.

Pause for thought

- Take a few moments to work out where on the scale in Figure 2.1 your everyday language about and towards others who are different to you tends to fall.

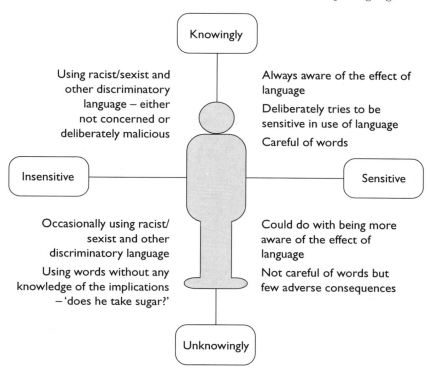

Knowingly

Using racist/sexist and other discriminatory language – either not concerned or deliberately malicious

Always aware of the effect of language

Deliberately tries to be sensitive in use of language

Careful of words

Insensitive

Sensitive

Occasionally using racist/ sexist and other discriminatory language

Using words without any knowledge of the implications – 'does he take sugar?'

Could do with being more aware of the effect of language

Not careful of words but few adverse consequences

Unknowingly

Figure 2.1   *Sensitivity and insensitivity may be either conscious or unconscious*

The diagram also illustrates a scale of extremes of consciousness of language. At one level you might really offend someone by what you say, but have absolutely no idea you are doing it, and at the other level people may take no offence at what you say, but you have no idea that there was an issue for you to avoid! Again, have a think about times when you may have unintentionally offended someone with what you have said.

An example of this might be where unintentional offence is often given to disabled people, where we refer to their 'courage' or use of phrases like 'wheelchair-bound'. Some disabled people find it intensely irritating at best and deeply offensive at worst to be patted on the head for courage in a situation which they cannot avoid, or to be referred to as wheelchair-bound when in fact the only thing that really disables them is the environment in which they live . . . buses with no ramps, no lifts at underground stations, and so on.

unintentional offence

Throughout this book we challenge you to consider the consequences of a particular action, word or thought. This is particularly important in the case of language. Ask yourself: 'What are the consequences of what I am saying, for the person or group to whom I am referring, the person I am speaking to, or for myself?'

Is one of the consequences of my language that it will give offence?

This test is obviously subjective and will depend on the way you view what is offensive or not, and how sensitive you are to the needs of other people. Even taking account of the problems of subjectivity, the benefit of asking such a question will be that you will automatically help yourself to avoid being unconsciously insensitive. It is hoped that by the time you have considered the issues in this book you will have developed greater sensitivity to what might be offensive.

test your use of language

It is also important to note that using offensive terminology, even when the target person or group is not present, can often reveal your true attitudes towards the issues. Terms like 'spade', 'coon', 'nigger', 'paki', 'Essex girl', 'queer', 'bender', 'poofter', 'nutter' – the list could go on – are *never* sensitively applied to people and should only be used in the context of exposing their offensiveness to others. Remember also that persistent use of such terms, for example at work, might put you in breach of the Race Relations or Sex Discrimination Act. The implications of this are discussed in Chapter 10.

some words are *never* appropriate

Pause for thought

- Are there any words that *you* routinely use that might cause offence?

Relevance

The second fundamental principle is that the words we use should be relevant. It is always worth asking, 'Do I need to use the word at all?' As we noted above, terms of downright abuse are only ever acceptably used in the context of exposing their offensiveness. Where, however, we are employing terms which are not in most contexts offensive, but nevertheless might have the effect of labelling a person or group (see below) then we do need to take special care.

is a 'grouping' label strictly necessary?

If we are talking about the issues surrounding community relations, we can hardly avoid using words which have the effect of grouping people – e.g. Bangladeshi, Pakistani, Jewish – but we do need to be careful, because in most other circumstances the term ceases to be relevant.

So if we are describing someone's suitability for promotion, praising someone who has done well, or complaining about bad behaviour, then it would not be relevant to use a grouping term which had nothing to do with what is being discussed.

This leads us to consider the relevance of using skin colour. Both the BBC and ITV currently run programmes which describe the scenes of crime and give out descriptions of suspects. When skin colour *is* relevant there is no particular problem in referring to it. When reporting crimes, it is becoming increasingly common to state a suspect's skin colour whether they are white *or* black, and to use both is of course important. If all descriptions of black suspects included the word 'black' but descriptions of white suspects did not include the word 'white' the effect would be to build a false association between 'black' and 'suspect' and not 'white' and 'suspect'. *Note, however, that skin colour alone does not amount to a description, neither is it always the most significant feature of a person.* If a bank robber wore a boiler suit, gloves and mask, there would be a number of factors for a witness to mention in any description other than skin colour!

skin colour does not amount to a description

LANGUAGE AND LABELLING

Amongst other uses, we use language to label things. Nouns (naming words) attached to objects, label them. In the same way, we have a tendency to label people and groups of people. The problem with this can be that the label takes on an importance out of all proportion to what it is trying to describe or name. Gordon Allport (1954), in his important book on prejudice, noted that some labels are 'exceedingly powerful'. In an example which, sadly, still has relevance more than 40 years on, he describes the experience of a man who had lost the sight of both eyes – a 'blind man'. 'There were many other ways', he reports, in which the man might have been described; as an expert typist, a careful listener, a good worker, and so on. In trying to get a job in the telephone order room of a department store, the man was confronted at his interview with: 'But you're a blind man'. The label 'blind man' had clouded the interviewer's judgement to the extent that all his other attributes became invisible.

Allport's views on labelling

'new age traveller' as a label

Labels have the effect of preventing any other classification of the person or group; yet no single label can ever describe all there is to know about a person. One label that has evolved in the early 1990s is 'new age traveller'. It is rarely meant to be just descriptive and even more rarely complimentary. A person to whom this label is applied is very often stereotyped by the rest of society as deviant, scrounging from the state, dirty, and so on. But is that *all* there is to know about new age travellers? Do they *all* scrounge from the state? Is there really *nothing* in their approach to life which is acceptable to society? The label has the effect of preventing most people from even considering these questions.

Pause for thought

- Take a moment to think about some of the labels you may use in the way you talk about other people and groups.

self-classification
is an important
guide

A general guide to the acceptability of a label is whether the person uses the term in relation to themselves

Groups often choose their own ways of classing themselves. Examples of this are when people say 'I'm black' or 'I'm Asian' or 'I'm a Muslim' or 'I'm a Christian' or 'I'm Turkish'. It's how people see themselves which counts, not how other groups want to label them. If the persons feels comfortable with using the term about themselves, the chances are they will not be offended if you use the term as well.

Nicknames

some nicknames
may not be
appropriate

Before we leave this point there is a case for caution to be made particularly in the area of nicknames. For example, if a black person found a particular racist nickname acceptable, and it was used regularly by colleagues, it could lead to real problems if those colleagues subsequently thought that they then had tacit approval to use the term in relation to other black people.

As we saw in Gordon Allport's example above, inappropriate labels are often attached to people with a disability. The fact is, of course, that a person is not the same as the condition they have. Some find it insensitive, for example, to refer to a person who has cerebral palsy as a 'spastic', or a person who has arthritis as an 'arthritic'. They are *people* who happen to have a condition which makes them less able to do certain things.

LANGUAGE AND HUMOUR

humour can be
a vehicle for
prejudice

We have found that in almost any discussion about equal opportunities one thing which is almost certain to come up is the subject of humour. This is probably not a bad thing, because inappropriate humour can have a very real effect in putting another group down and needs to be dealt with. If we are really developing a greater sensitivity to the needs and feelings of others, the 'Englishman, Irishman and Scotsman' jokes will become less and less funny, as will all jokes made at the expense of others such as people who are gay or lesbian, members of minority ethnic groups, women, or people who have a disability.

Psychologists and sociologists have tried with great difficulty to pin down the real essence of humour. 'What can be said with some certainty, however, is that we *can* observe not so much what it is, but the effect it has. Some of the functions of humour are outlined by Hugh Foot (in Hargie, 1986), and they are worth noting because they are directly relevant to arguments about humour in equal opportunities. The uses of humour he identifies include:

Expression of liking and friendship

Many people seem to value humour as a social asset. They use it as a way of gauging how people are responding to them, and a shared sense of humour can help to oil the wheels of social interaction. One key point here is that because humour is so valued, jokes will often be made by someone who is seeking the approval of others. This is important to remember in equal opportunities, because a person from a minority group might well go along with jokes about themselves and their group not because they agree with the jokes, or are not hurt by them, but because if they don't, they will fail to conform to a social asset that is valued.

humour as a social asset

Expression of dislike and hostility

There is little doubt that a great deal of humour is cruel, in that it is aimed at oddities, low intelligence, unusual habits or (in the eyes of the joker) negative features about a person; very often things that they cannot change. Hugh Foot argues that humour might well be the only socially acceptable way of expressing hostility. At one end of the scale we might take pleasure and laugh at someone slipping on a banana skin, whereas at the other we might use jokes to express our outright hostility to minority ethnic groups and others who are in some way different from the majority.

. . . as an expression of hostility

Controlling social interaction

Humour is often used to change the direction or depth of a particular conversation. There are, of course, many times when such a use would be perfectly legitimate, but very often it is used as a device to divert attention from issues which are becoming uncomfortable. This is a very frequent phenomenon in equal opportunities training. It is not at all uncommon to find that as soon as the going gets tough and deep-seated attitudes are being addressed, someone will crack a joke in an attempt to make themselves and the group feel more comfortable.

. . . as a device to avoid discomfort

Reinforcing stereotypes

Foot argues that 'the power of humour in perpetuating myths and reinforcing stereotyped and traditional attitudes is greatly underestimated'. 'How else', he asks, 'do we derive our stereotyped views about the Irish, the Scots, the Welsh, Protestants, Jews or Catholics?' This leads us to discuss the myth that is central to all this, and to outline some of the arguments against it.

. . . as a reinforcer of stereotypes

Myth

'I was only joking.'

Myth-buster

- In terms of the law on equal opportunities there are numerous examples of how jokes can amount to either racial or sexual harassment. It doesn't matter that you were joking, it is how the other person *receives* the joke that is important. So it's quite possible that your joke might actually be amounting to unfair treatment of the other person.
- A reinforcement to the 'I was only joking' excuse is the argument that people often laugh at themselves, and that this therefore justifies humour at their expense. Now it would of course be wrong to suggest that people never laugh at themselves, of course they do; but what we need to ask when this is happening is, 'who holds the power?'. If the person making the joke is in the dominant group, whether it be ethnic, gender, sexuality or physically able, then what options does the person in the minority have?
- They can run the risk of not laughing and seeming to be spoilsports, making themselves even less attractive to the dominant group. Or they can go along with the joke, find it funny (even if they don't) and by giving *way* if not gain acceptance, then at least avoid further ridicule. The poet Lord Byron seems to have summed the situation up in the line: 'And if I laugh at any mortal thing, 'Tis that I may not weep' *(Don Juan)*.

LANGUAGE WHICH EXCLUDES

One sure way of telling if a person is serious in their efforts to treat people fairly by the application of equal opportunities is to listen to the way that they speak or write. Now one thing we need to stress is that we all make mistakes and that we need to get our own houses in order before we start jumping down other people's throats and pointing out the deficiencies of their words. Having said that, as we grow more sensitive to the important role language can play in treating people fairly, it is likely that we will more frequently notice words and phrases that clearly exclude some groups, assert male dominance or put others down. It probably won't be long before someone accuses you of nit-picking, or making a mountain out of a molehill. We all need to remember that we are dealing with a real problem, not just a politically correct issue. There are three issues that will arise most frequently.

mistakes will happen . . . as we become more sensitive

Words which exclude women

In the English language, there seems to be an assumption that the world is male, and although words like 'mankind' have been traditionally *supposed* to refer to both men and women, the image that is conjured up for most people seems to be male, even though in the UK there are, in fact, more women than men in the population! If language is to be both sensitive and relevant, and if we are really going to try and promote positive images and acknowledge the contribution of women to our society, then terms which exclude women must be avoided. You can probably think of lots of examples of what has become known as 'gender-specific language', but here are a few specific occupational examples which will give you a head start.

male-dominated concepts

chairman	=	chair
charwoman	=	cleaner
fireman	=	firefighter
foreman	=	supervisor
headmaster	=	headteacher
layman		lay person
manpower	=	human resources, staff
policeman		police officer
taxman	=	tax officer/inspector
workmanlike	=	proficient/professional
workmen	=	workers

Using 'he' or 'she'

Many valiant attempts have been made to try to solve this one, and opinion is divided as to which is the best option. In writing this book we have tried to avoid the problem by writing round it. Sometimes the grammar may not be to the liking of a strict grammarian, but the alternatives have their difficulties too. Many people find 'he/she', '(s)he' or 's/he' to be clumsy and difficult to read. Others use he throughout their writing and put a disclaimer at the front to the effect that the word is to be taken to include she, as has traditionally been the case. We find this alternative a bit thin as it still has overtones of male dominance. Why, for example, could 'she' not include 'he' – which, in terms of the letters, it does?! Yet another method is to use he in one chapter and she in the next, and so on. This also has its drawbacks and has been known to confuse readers. You must make your own decision, but whatever you decide, be aware of the problem and be sensitive in your use of language.

the problem of he/she

Using modifiers

Be careful of modifying a word to give it a meaning other than the one you actually intend. It is rarely relevant and often insensitive to say 'woman doctor', 'woman police officer', or 'male nurse', as these uses suggest that there is something special or unique about being a woman (or man) in those roles. Ask yourself 'why would I not say "male doctor"?', and so on.

gender as a
qualifying word

We rarely refer to males over 18 as 'boys', but describe them as young men. Why then are females over 18 so often referred to as 'girls'? There is a strong sense of implied dominance in such language and it is best avoided.

PARTICULAR WORDS AND PHRASES

language is
constantly
changing

Language is a dynamic thing in that it changes all the time. At the time of writing this book children seem to use 'wicked' or 'bad' to mean 'brilliant' or 'wonderful'! You can no doubt think of examples of words that had special meaning in your own youth, or if you are a reader who still considers yourself young, you will know of such words in common currency! So it is with the language of equal opportunities. Many people, in their efforts to treat people fairly, are now being more sensitive and appropriate in what they say and are accepting that words matter.

'political
correctness?'

There is another phrase which is being used more and more, namely 'political correctness'. It has taken on a meaning which seems to denigrate efforts to be more sensitive and appropriate in the use of language. While the phrase might fairly be used in relation to extremists, we believe that it is often used as a smokescreen by those who feel threatened by a challenge to their own use of language, and who demonstrate an unwillingness to change.

Pause for thought

- If you were asked what you understand by the term 'political correctness' what would you say?
- Is it a helpful or unhelpful concept?

Words to use with caution

In the following list, we offer some words which, if not avoided altogether, need more careful consideration about the way they are used.

Before starting the list it is worth noting that there have been a number of spoof 'dictionaries' and rewritten fairy stories which attempt humour by advancing 'politically correct' language as a joke. Remember that any humour they contain is at the expense of genuine attempts to achieve fair use of language.

Black

So-called racial categories in most common use do not refer to race at all but to the colour of a person's skin. If you refer to the guidelines above, you will note that using skin colour is appropriate sometimes, either as a means of identifying an individual, provided generalized stereotypes such as coloured are avoided, or because the group in question has chosen that as a self-classification. Black Caucus, Black Churches, Black Music are just three examples of the latter. On the other hand there are many words and phrases in everyday use that continue to reinforce negative images of certain groups. Such words and phrases as black mark, black-leg, black cloud, black as the devil, black sheep, black death and blackmail all refer to things which are not good, and perpetuate false images of blackness.

Coloured

This term is still often used by white people in Britain, and many to whom it is applied find it at best patronizing and at worst racist. There are links with the former South African apartheid system, which classified some citizens as coloured. As a form of identification it has no value as it is too non-specific. It is also a term sometimes used in the Caribbean as a derogatory description of someone of dual ethnic background.

Crippled by

Also 'suffering from', 'struck down with' and 'afflicted by'. If it is necessary to refer to the person's condition at all, just use 'has', 'had' or 'with'.

Disabled

Using the word as a noun implies that the disabled are a group set apart from the rest of society. Throughout this guide we will emphasize that people are individuals and should be treated as such. If it is necessary to refer to it at all, 'person with a disability' may be more sensitive.

Girlie

Seemingly growing in use, the term implies a host of inappropriate and patronizing images.

Handicapped

This word is rarely appropriately applied to a person with a disability, unless it is qualified in some way. A person may be handicapped *by* something, such as an illness or disability. Of course they may be giving you a head start at golf! The word originated many years ago in horse-racing, where the rider of a particularly good horse was required to ride with a cap in one hand, to give the other riders an advantage. This cap-in-hand image is seen by some as implying that disabled people or people with a handicap should need to depend on charity for their well-being, and they, not surprisingly, find this offensive.

Homosexual

The term is in less frequent use these days and is not usually favoured by the people to whom it is applied. The word is medical in origin and, when it is used, often only means men. Again, where it is necessary to make reference to a person's sexual orientation, it is better to use the term gay man, lesbian, or member of the gay community.

Immigrant

This is usually an inappropriate term to use as it has implications that the person is somehow an outsider, or an intruder into society. The term has also generally been used to refer to a black immigrant and therefore reinforces prejudice against a particular group. In fact, about half of the British non-white population was born in the UK. The term may be used appropriately when a person's status under the legislation relating to immigration is under question.

Invalid

Use 'disabled person', 'person with a disability', or 'person who is less able'.

Mental handicap

It is often preferable to replace this with 'person with special needs'.

Negro, Caucasian, Negroid, Oriental

These are all words which are becoming redundant in our language. They are terms relating to discredited theories of racial origin which held that there were valid biological differences between people of different races. The only significant biological differences among the human species are those of medical relevance – such as blood groupings – which are not distributed according to skin colour at all.

Settler

If it becomes necessary to refer to the fact that a person originated overseas, then 'settler' is a term with fewer connotations. The word implies full immigration rights, which are enjoyed by the vast majority of people in question.

Victim

Use 'person who has', 'person with', or 'person who has experienced'.

Wheelchair-bound

Use 'wheelchair user'. As we will see in Chapter 7, the main thing that makes wheelchair users *bound* is the environment in which they have to live and move.

KEY POINTS IN THIS CHAPTER

- Language has a vital role to play in treating people fairly (or unfairly).
- Words should be sensitive and relevant.
- 'I was only joking', is a thinly veiled excuse for unfairness.
- Labels obscure all the other qualities a person has.
- Your spoken and written language will be a test of your commitment to fairness.
- There are some words and phrases which need special care in their use, and may be best avoided altogether.

PERSONAL ACTION PLAN

Try answering the following questions:

How will the things I have learnt in this chapter change the way I think and act towards others who are different to me?

What has this chapter helped me to learn about myself with regard to:

- my beliefs;
- my attitudes;
- my values;
- my knowledge of others;
- my behaviour;
- my use of language;
- my responsibilities;
- the way I see the world?

How do I need to change in order to become:

- fairer;
- more sensitive;
- more understanding;
- less prejudicial;
- less discriminatory;
- better able to deal with people according to their needs?

If I were to change one thing about the way I act as a result of reading this chapter what would it be?

Chapter 3

Being in a Majority Group

We are going to be discussing what it means to be part of a majority group and equally what it's like to be on the outside of a majority group. By looking at this important area, we hope to show that the ways in which members of majority groups think about and behave towards other people who are not in that group tend to disadvantage and discriminate against those on the 'outside'.

By the time you have read this chapter you should have a better understanding of:

- the relationship between British culture and different minority groups;
- how the face of British culture has changed and continues to change;
- how ideas about what is normal can create prejudice and unfairness;
- the part that members of majority groups play in deciding what is normal;
- how thinking in terms of 'us and them' reinforces differences and prejudice;
- what it means to be in a majority group; and
- what it means to be on the outside of a majority group.

BRITISH CULTURE

Pause for thought

Take a few minutes to think about the whole idea of being British and about British culture and traditions. Then try to answer the following questions.

- What does the idea of being British mean to you personally?
- Who decides what British culture should be like?
- Can you think of ways in which British culture has changed or is changing?

Don't worry too much about what the word 'culture' actually means. The truth is that there is no hard and fast definition, and different people will probably come up with different examples of what culture is if asked. The important thing for this exercise is that you start to think about what British culture means to *you*.

Being British

Let's take each of these questions in turn. The first thing we asked you was: *what does the idea of being British mean to you?* Certainly the word 'British' just on its own can carry all sorts of meanings for all sorts of people. But whatever those different meanings and ideas might be, the chances are that the word suggests certain characteristics which people who think themselves British share. A common language perhaps, the fact that they live in the UK, the type of food they eat or the clothes they wear, the type of education they have received, a common history, or even the type of TV programmes they watch.

what does the idea of being British mean to you?

These characteristics may well be part of what being British actually is, but when you start to look closely at them they don't always hold up that well. Do I have to live in the UK to be British? If that *were* the case British people who lived abroad would no longer be able to consider themselves as British! What about the food we eat? Some of the most popular types of food in the UK, like burgers, pizza and curry, don't fit that easily with the 'roast beef and yorkshire pudding' or 'fish and chips' image of British cuisine. There are so many different examples of how what is thought to be culturally normal is actually *relative and changing*.

What *is* important for our purposes when thinking about equal opportunities and fair treatment is how these images of Britishness can be used to *exclude* members of our community. For example, the fact that a woman member of the community wears a sari and (because English is her second language) may not speak English fluently, can lead some people to believe that she cannot or should not be considered British. The fact that those same misguided people do things themselves or have characteristics which also break away from what is culturally 'normal' or typical is forgotten.

images of 'Britishness' can exclude some minorities

How British culture can exclude

This brings us to the second question: *who decides what British culture should be like?* Let's face this question head-on without pulling our punches! It is the white, heterosexual, male majority with access to forms of power (particularly political power) in our community who have established and who continue to define what is to be considered culturally typical or normal. They hold the monopoly on British culture and what it means. If you don't easily fit into their definitions you could find yourself looking at the majority group from the outside, with all that this entails.

those with power tend to determine how things are

Black people, women, people with disabilities, single parents, members of the gay community, all of these people and others can, at certain times, find themselves marginalized (pushed to the edge of our society) and isolated in some way from the majority. They don't fit in with the image of what being a normal and typical British person is, an image that has been created by the powerful majority. This may show itself in the way that members of the majority group talk about and behave towards members of these other

the majority tends to marginalize the minority

groups or it may reveal itself in a closing down of opportunities enjoyed by the majority, such as poorer education, restricted opportunities for work, lack of promotion or a lack of access to services and facilities.

Returning to our discussion about the common roots of prejudice covered in Chapter 1, you will recall that we spoke about power and vulnerability. In the circumstances just described, you can readily see how these two common roots of prejudice operate. Members of the majority group with the power to say what British culture is and should continue to be; and what the normal and typical British citizen is like, use this power to exclude people who, by virtue of the fact that they are in some way different from the majority, appear to threaten the majority group's hold on power.

perceived threats may be . . .

- In the case of gay men and lesbians, this threat is a moral one, a perceived attack on how the majority define right, good and proper ways of behaving. 'If we allow gay men and lesbians to function as full and respected members of our community, we will be forced to rethink our values on sexual preference and normality, and of what is right and proper behaviour.'

. . . to morality

- In the case of black people, this threat is to aspects of white dominance and white culture. 'If we allow black people to become full and respected members of our community, with equal rights and opportunities, they will rise to positions of influence and power and we will lose our places as the people with the influence and control.'

. . . to culture

- In the case of women, it is a threat to male dominance and male power. 'If we allow women to have equal power and opportunities, in our culture they will rise to positions of influence and power, men might then have to take over some of the domestic responsibilities!'

. . . to power

- In the case of people with disabilities, it is a threat to majority views of normality and ability. 'If we allow people with a disability to be considered full and respected members of the community, it would show them to be equally capable of doing the things that we have argued you need to be fully able to do. We may also have to adjust our own environment to take account of their needs and that would be expensive.'

. . . to normality and ability

In each of these cases the power of the majority group is used to overcome their own feelings of vulnerability and to address what they see as threats to their vested interest and to the status quo (how things are).

How British culture can change

The third question we asked you to consider was: *can you think of ways in which British culture has changed or is changing?* This is an important question as it allows us to identify not only the changes to British culture itself but also the consequences of that change.

For example, during the 1950s, the law which had made homosexual acts between consenting males above the age of 21 years an offence was abolished. This change marked a new degree of social tolerance, which has been added to recently by the lowering of the age of consent for gay men to 18 years. Calls for its further reduction to 16 years, to make it consistent with the heterosexual age of consent, continue to be discussed in parliament. This change to the law suggests an increased desire to treat members of the gay community with a greater degree of equality and fairness.

Other significant changes include the gradual realization that our built environment and public transport systems disadvantage people with disabilities. This cultural change may lead to new buildings and forms of transport which everyone can use easily. Making provision for people with disabilities *adds* to the usefulness of buildings and transport – it does not make such facilities any less useful to the fully able. Examples include the widening of aisles in shops, which helps parents with children in pushchairs just as much as those who use a wheelchair. Lifts are similarly helpful.

Further examples include the selection of black candidates (particularly in the Labour Party) which has led to members of the black community becoming Members of Parliament. There is a slowly growing number of black people achieving positions of power and influence in our community such as judges and trades union leaders. We could also mention the growing popularity of the Notting Hill Carnival, which has become a highlight of the British social calendar. This points towards increased awareness of and interest in aspects of black British life and British/Afro-Caribbean culture.

> **Pause for thought**
>
> - Try to think of more examples of how British culture might be changing for the better.
> - Focus on where you work and live: what change is still needed?

British culture has been, and is, changing

BEING NORMAL

If someone who didn't know you was speaking to you on the telephone and during the conversation they asked you to describe yourself and to tell them a bit about who you are and what you're like, what would you say in reply? Difficult, isn't it? How do you decide what's relevant and interesting, what to say and what to leave out?

We have run this type of exercise with students over many years, with some interesting results. What tends to be most interesting though, is not what people say but what they don't say! White students rarely tend to say 'I'm white', whereas black students often include this fact. Heterosexuals

how do you describe yourself?

never say 'I'm straight', but gay men and women who have come out might include the fact that they are gay. What people say about themselves can tell us a lot about what *they* believe is important about themselves and what marks out their individuality. What they don't tend to say is what they consider to be normal and thus uninteresting. They are so used to the normal bits of their identity that those bits become invisible to them, by and large.

If you live in a predominantly white community the fact that you are white will fade into the background because you are rarely, if ever, reminded of that fact. After all, you are unlikely to be refused a job or a house because of your colour. However, if you are black and live in a largely white community, you are more likely to be reminded of that fact because of the ways in which members of the majority group behave towards you and because of the restricted opportunities available to you. As such, the answer to the question 'what's normal?' is 'what the people in the majority group are'.

Does it matter? To answer this question, imagine you have a disability of some kind. Because the majority of people are able-bodied, everything around them is arranged to meet their needs – try and travel on the London Underground if you are a wheelchair user, for example, or try making a phone call from a public phone-box if you are deaf. The same type of problems can arise for any section of the community who differ from the majority in some way – it won't be long before they are reminded of this difference.

most people see 'normal' in terms of the majority group's definition

---

Pause for thought

Try a little bit of honest reflective thinking here by answering these questions:

- Can you identify your own ideas and attitudes about what you consider to be normal in the areas of physical ability, colour or sexuality?
- Can you remember a situation in which your views of what is normal may have excluded certain people or groups of people?
- Have you been in a position where you were made to feel other than normal by someone else? If so how did this feel?

Another important point about attitudes concerning what is normal is that they tend to make the majority feel safe and comfortable, like members of the same club who will stick together against common threats. In fact, the idea of club membership provides a good example of ways in which women become excluded from certain male-dominated institutions. There still remain many male-only clubs and organizations, such as the Freemasons and Gentlemen's clubs, whose rules strictly forbid women joining. In other aspects of life women's exclusion is ensured by informal means, for example by ridiculing girls who want to play football.

In fact, images of what is normal surround us every day. Adverts in magazines and on television provide strong and appealing images which often depict normal family life as a white, middle-class, 'three-bed-suburban-semi' type of existence. Mum is at home desperately trying to decide between competing washing powders in order to wash Jimmy's rugby shorts. Upstairs her teenage daughter dresses like a model from *Vogue* while dad, a grey-suited successful businessman, does what normal men do: he flirts, drinks and succeeds. It's easy to dismiss these pre-packaged images as advertising hype, but they invade and inform our views of normality in subtle ways which we pick up often without realizing. These images of what's normal reinforce our stereotypes of gender, relationships and ethnicity.

the media perpetuate images of 'normality'

US AND THEM

You will have realized by now that ideas and opinions about what is normal are not fixed in stone and are not self-evident truths! Instead they are based upon traditional ways of seeing the world and thinking about people, views and ideas which are controlled by the majority group. By saying what should be considered normal, the majority group sets about creating difference and division amongst members of the community, and this difference and division leads to an 'us and them' situation in which the 'us' is the majority group and the 'them' becomes represented by various other 'out-groups'.

in reality, normality is not fixed in concrete

This type of 'us and them' thinking lies at the heart of prejudice and often crops up in the arguments of people who are attempting to justify their own prejudiced attitudes and values, let's look at a few examples:

'The problem is *they* want careers and within two years *they* have left to have a baby.'

'*They* want to be part of our society but *they* stick together, wearing weird clothes and eating all that smelly food.'

'them and us' arguments

'*They* hang around on street corners moaning about not having work whilst the rest of *us* have to knuckle down.'

What messages are the people making these comments sending out about their views of themselves and their views of other people?

In Chapter 2 we took quite a detailed look at the whole area of the type of language we use and the messages we send to others. Many of the skills and ideas contained within that section are applicable here when thinking about how we often use 'them' and 'they' when talking about people who are different from 'us'. Be aware of the implied meanings and consequences of using these terms.

IN-GROUPS AND OUT-GROUPS

Your own experience

So far, we have looked at majority groups in terms of their power to influence cultural norms (by cultural norms we mean ideas and attitudes about what is considered normal and acceptable within a particular culture). But if we want to change this type of large-scale thinking and stereotyping and prevent individuals from becoming excluded and isolated, we need to begin at the personal level by realizing how we, as individuals, may be contributing to such thinking and behaviour.

Pause for thought

Try and identify a time when you felt in the minority or on the outside of a group. Perhaps you were the only man in a group of women, or the only woman in a group of men. Or maybe you were the only white person within a group of black people or the only black person in a group of white people. Alternatively, you may have found yourself a stranger in a group of people all of whom knew each other well. Whatever the situation was, we want you to try and answer these questions:

- How did it feel being in the minority or on the outside of the 'in-group'?
- What was it about the 'in-group' that made you feel in the minority or on the outside?
- Did the way that members of the 'in-group' behaved towards you make you feel more isolated or less?
- Did you change your behaviour at all in order to become more acceptable to the 'in-group'?
- Did you feel you had to prove yourself to members of the 'in-group' to become accepted?
- Did you feel that members of the 'in-group' exaggerated the things that they shared as a group when you were around them?

It's extremely useful to be able to identify the thoughts and feelings that *you* had as a member of the 'out-group' in such situations, as this will increase your ability to use empathy towards others when the situation is reversed and you find yourself the member of an 'in-group' and they are outside your group (members of the 'out-group'). By realizing how you felt in this situation you will realize how they are probably feeling in the same or similar situations.

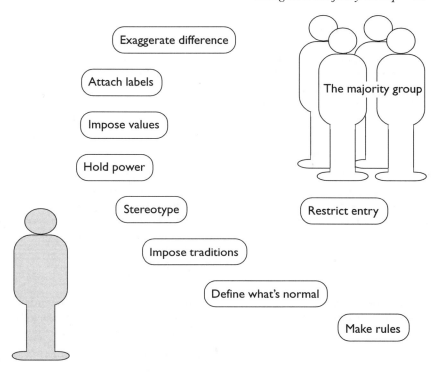

Figure 3.1 *Ways in which the majority group keep control and hold power over minority groups*

'In-groups' use all sorts of strategies in order to keep other people out (see Figure 3.1). They may ignore the outsider, make jokes about them or the group they are perceived to belong to, or say derogatory things about them either behind their backs or within earshot, but not directly to them. Members of the 'in-group' may exaggerate things they hold in common or crack 'in-jokes', or they may socialize together in ways that exclude the outsider. Alternatively, they may patronize the person, saying how brave the person is to want to join the 'in-group' at all, or they may make the person their token representative from the 'out-group', seeking their 'out-group' views.

the effects of in-groups and out-groups

In many of these situations the 'out-group' person has only a limited number of choices: join in and conform to 'in-group' attitudes, stereotyping and prejudices by trying to 'become' one of the 'in-group'; keep quiet in the hope that members of the 'in-group' will get tired and lose interest; or confront and challenge.

As we said in Chapter 1, there can often be enormous pressure placed on people to conform to the majority viewpoint by accepting that the majority

pressure to
conform . . .

. . . an example

view of things is the correct one. Let's look at an example of how this might occur in practice.

A woman joins a company with high expectations that she will be able to rise through the firm using her own abilities and merits. She soon discovers that, as a woman, she is a member of an 'out-group'. When confronted by sexism and male pressure, she is forced either to change her expectations or to leave. By conforming she will be accepting the 'in-group' (in this case male-majority) view that women are not equal workers with equal rights to men.

In the same situation, as we have said, she might instead choose to resist such prejudice by setting out to prove that she is as capable, if not more so, than her male counterpart and in this way, she responds to a feeling that she must be better than her male colleagues in order to compete with them on an equal level. Typically, in such situations, the 'in-group' male workers will close ranks, exaggerating their common values and interests.

Pause for thought

Consider these groups in our community: women, gay men and lesbians, people who have a disability, members of the black community – then try to think of examples of the following:

- Ways in which members of these groups are excluded from the majority group.
- Ways in which you as an individual may have contributed (even in a small way) to their being excluded.

If you can, try not to re-use examples that we have already supplied in the parts of the book you have read.

KEY POINTS IN THIS CHAPTER

- Ideas about what is *typical* and *normal* in our society are *relative and changing*.
- Attitudes and opinions about what British culture is and should be like and who should be considered a normal British person serve to *exclude and isolate* certain members of our community.
- British culture is constantly changing, revealing changes in the way that different groups and individuals are viewed. Some of these changes promote fair treatment and equal opportunities; others attack it.
- Aspects of your self-identity which you consider normal often become invisible to you, whereas things which are shown to be different about you become important.

- Ideas about what and who is normal are controlled by the majority group and serve to divide people and groups. Those who are not considered normal become disadvantaged and isolated by the majority.
- The majority group uses its control over definitions of what is normal to safeguard its own positions and interests.
- The terms 'us and them' reinforce divisions in our community and differences between people. Such words often crop up in prejudiced language.
- Each of us at some time or other has had experience of being in an 'out-group' with the feelings of isolation and vulnerability which result. By identifying and understanding these feelings we will be in a better position to extend empathy to others when the situation is reversed.
- 'In-groups' use many different strategies towards 'out-group' members in order to retain their power over them. These strategies restrict how the 'out-group' person can act.

PERSONAL ACTION PLAN

Try answering the following questions:

How will the things I have learnt in this chapter change the way I think and act towards others who are different to me?

What has this chapter helped me to learn about myself with regard to:

- my beliefs;
- my attitudes;
- my values;
- my knowledge of others;
- my behaviour;
- my use of language;
- my responsibilities;
- the way I see the world?

How do I need to change in order to become:

- fairer;
- more sensitive;
- more understanding;
- less prejudicial;
- less discriminatory;
- better able to deal with people according to their needs?

If I were to change one thing about the way I act as a result of reading this chapter what would it be?

Chapter 4

Racism

Racism is a major problem in this country and continues to affect the lives of large sections of our community. This chapter will focus on some of the key issues in this important area and will ask you questions about your own opinions and attitudes along the way. By the time you have finished reading through this chapter we hope you will have a better idea of what you think about:

- ideas of 'race' and the meaning of the word 'racism';
- institutional and personal racism; how it arises and the ways in which this country still has a long way to go to eradicate it;
- how the effects of institutional racism can be seen in the areas of employment, education and housing and other parts of the social system;
- something of what it means to be white, and the issues which go with assumptions that being white is to be normal; and
- some of the myths which crop up when thinking about racism, and how they can be exploded.

INTRODUCTION

Right from the beginning of this book we have emphasized that prejudice and discrimination flow out of the negative attitudes and beliefs that people hold about others who are different from themselves. People on the receiving end of such prejudice could not do anything about being different, even if they wanted to.

In the case of racism, the differences which give rise to prejudice are mostly to do with the colour of a person's skin and the cultural beliefs that others believe (stereotypically) such people must hold. If racism is all about prejudice and discrimination against people because of their colour, what do those who hold racist attitudes want black people to do – become white? Clearly this is not only insulting but impossible. It's like disliking someone because they have brown eyes and you only like people with blue eyes! This may sound silly, but racism *is* as illogical and simplistic as that.

But while people who have black skin cannot (and don't want to) change their colour, people who hold racist attitudes can (and should) change these attitudes. In fact, when you think about it this argument holds true for all

prejudice in racism is largely based on skin colour and culture

racism is illogical

forms of prejudice. What *can* be changed are the ideas, beliefs, opinions and attitudes that assert that people who are different from the majority (whether black, gay or those with disabilities) are somehow lesser citizens.

The whole issue of racism gives rise to many myths. Accordingly this chapter contains more myth-busters than others in this book. To make it easier to get at them, we have grouped all the myth-busters at the end of the chapter.

Another issue to be aware of as you read this chapter is that the whole subject of racism can often prove very emotive. This has certainly been our experience – racism, more than any other area within equal opportunities, has the potential to get people really 'steamed up'. In fact you might find yourself feeling uncomfortable or even defensive – that's OK, use these feelings as a way of increasing your own awareness of the issues you personally find challenging. All we ask is that you approach these issues with an open mind and a willingness to challenge your own behaviour and to think where such challenge is needed.

racism is usually an emotive subject

RACE, ETHNICITY AND RACISM

The idea of race

From the start we need to deal with what might appear to be an inconsistency, if not a contradiction, in the way we use the word 'race'. The term is often used to refer to groups of people with specific and clearly identifiable common characteristics. Increasingly, this view has been challenged as inaccurate and inadequate. At the same time, you will see the word crop up in discussions about equal opportunities – for instance, we have the Commission for Racial Equality and the Race Relations Act. The reason for this is that many of the mechanisms put in place to combat racism embody the term 'race' in their titles as a way of showing that they are working *against* prejudice and discrimination on the grounds of ethnicity or colour.

One event in recent history in which the concept of race was challenged occurred in 1964, when 20 leading scientists were brought together by the United Nations Educational Scientific and Cultural Organization (UNESCO) to consider the issue of race. Most of these scientists were anthropologists, but their number also included specialists in the field of population genetics and haematology (the study of blood). Their agreed statement concluded that all humans living today belong to a *single species*. Humankind *cannot* (and indeed should not) be classified into clear-cut categories, even if some might wish to do so (Banton, 1973).

humans are a single species

Now we are not suggesting that just because one group of scientists got together, that wraps the argument up. What we are suggesting, however, is that the UNESCO meeting was typical of the way thinking about race has developed.

Some features to emerge from the change in thinking about the very idea of race include the following:

- Differences between individuals *within* a so-called racial grouping are often much more marked than the average differences *between* those groupings.
- The characteristics of individuals very often do not in fact correspond with those of their supposed racial type. The latter characteristics turn out to be gross stereotypes.
- There is *absolutely no* biological justification for speaking of any racial grouping as being superior to any other.
- Presumed differences in the level of achievement between groupings of people are solely related to the *social and cultural development* of those groups and to subjective views of what constitutes 'achievement'.

culture is
learned, not
inherited

We cannot escape the fact, of course, that populations do differ in form, physical appearance and culture. These differences, however, are really just the results of selection processes and adaptations which have taken place over centuries in response to different environmental conditions and climates. The physical form and characteristics of our parents may be hereditary for us, but we do not inherit their culture (as was believed by those who subscribed to the theory that a person's race dictated their culture). Culture is *learnt*.

To sum up, we cannot stress too highly that human beings cannot be biologically grouped as races in any meaningful way. Grouping in other ways, such as by blood type, of course, cross all racial and ethnic boundaries.

We are all members of the human race, a single species deserving equal rights and opportunities.

We cannot make this point better than it is made in the United Nations Universal Declaration of Human Rights:

ARTICLE 1 'All human beings are born free and equal in dignity and rights . . .'

ARTICLE 2 'Everyone is entitled to all rights and freedoms set forth in this Declaration, without distinction of any kind, such as race, colour, sex, language, religion, political or other opinion, national or social origin, property, birth or other status.'

You will notice that the Declaration itself uses the word 'race'. As we have seen, the word can be very misleading in its implication that there are fundamental, significant differences between groups of human beings. Rather than use this term, with the danger of its historical associations of biological superiority of one race over another, we need to try and find an alternative. It is usually preferable to use the alternative term *'ethnic group'*, as anthropologists now do. This description is more helpful in that it describes a social group which is held together not only by common kinship, but also by its culture and/or religion (Calvert and Calvert, 1992).

'ethnic group' is a more useful term

Pause for thought

A recent government report on the state of equal opportunities training in the police was given the title

Winning the Race

- Based on what you have learned so far about appropriate use of language, race and sensitivity, what are your thoughts and feelings about this title?

The word 'ethnic' comes from the Greek word *ethne*, which means tribe, and this is important because just as with religions, nearly all tribes have procedures for incorporating new members into their group and excluding others as 'outsiders'. In Chapter 3 we spoke at length about how British culture is shaped and controlled by the majority group, and about the difficulties this poses for members of other groups who want to integrate. These cultural criteria (the norms and values of British culture – dress, accent, background, diet, traditions, etc) are 'tribal' procedures for incorporating new members into the group and excluding others.

Everybody is a member of an ethnic group, and it is important to remember this to avoid a 'them and us' viewpoint or to avoid using the term ethnic in a derogatory way which suggests that 'ethnics' are other than 'us', somehow separate, perhaps foreign to our customs and way of life. *We all have ethnicity* – it is just that in this country some ethnic groups are in the minority and others are not. It follows, therefore, that although we use the term 'racism' to describe prejudices and discriminations based on the fact that a person is a member of a different (perhaps minority) ethnic group, it would probably be more accurate to term this 'ethnism'. However, we will continue to use the term 'racism' as its meaning is generally understood and accepted.

we all have ethnicity

The tragedy of viewing minority ethnic communities as undesirable outsiders is that when such racism exists, humans invariably suffer. History is littered with examples of how human beings have suffered and continue to suffer at the hands of those who wish to pursue a policy of segregation and 'purity' of racial extraction. One need only reflect upon the so-called 'ethnic cleansing' in the territory of former Yugoslavia to see this.

Racism

Pause for thought

- Take a moment to consider what *you* think racism is. You may even have been a victim of it. How closely do the definitions below match with your own?
- How important do you feel it is to define what racism is?

Having run many training courses aimed at raising awareness of racism and its consequences, we have often had students question the importance of definitions of racism and racial prejudice. What we encourage them to realize is that unless people measure their own attitudes and behaviour against an agreed and shared standard (in the case of training such agreement is, of course, group agreement) it becomes all too easy for people to 'duck-and-dive' their own prejudices by simply inventing their own definitions of what racism amounts to.

Because of this fact, we will look in some detail at the meaning of words, terms and definitions as these relate to racism, in order that you (the reader) can reflect on your position and viewpoint with reference to them.

Racialism

To hold a belief that 'races' have distinctive characteristics, determined by hereditary factors which endow some 'races' with in-built superiority over others, is called 'racialism'. We hope we have shown you that such a viewpoint is not only invalid but can easily underpin racist views.

Racism

To believe that discrimination against a person on the basis of race (or ethnic grouping) is justified is called 'racism'. Two attempts at defining racism that we have come across are:

- Racism is 'decisions and policies made on consideration of race, for the purpose of subordinating a minority ethnic group and maintaining control over that group'.
- Racism is the combination of 'prejudice and power' (by power we mean the power to put that racism into practice).

attitudes *and* behaviour make up racism

When we (the authors) speak about racism we take it to include not only racist behaviour but also racist attitudes. We have lost count of the number of times we have heard people say that they feel comfortable with holding what amount to racist attitudes, but that such attitudes never become translated into action.

	DISCRIMINATION	NON-DISCRIMINATION
INTENTIONAL	Aim to make this area as small as possible, or eliminate it completely	This is where you can become more sensitive through greater awareness
UNINTENTIONAL	Aim, as an active reflector on your behaviour, to be more aware of when this happens	It becomes second nature to treat people equally without consciously having to try

Figure 4.1 *Use this grid to help you sort out whether there are areas of your behaviour and thinking that you need to challenge*

For a start, our attitudes are constantly being given voice by what we say and do in all sorts of different, and often subtle, ways. We have often been involved in an equal opportunities training course where a participant has felt comfortable to express aspects of their racism in front of a member of a minority ethnic group, and in the same breath go on to say it would never affect their behaviour. Such people fail to realize that behaviour includes:

- what they say;
- how they say it;
- jokes;
- the type of language they use;
- throw-away comments;
- asides;

and a variety of other forms of both verbal and non-verbal (sometimes called body language) behaviour.

Intentional and unintentional personal racism

A major problem with much early anti-racist training during the late 1970s and early 1980s was that it took the position that everybody was intentionally racist in some way. Not surprisingly many well-intentioned people became very offended by this and, far from learning from such training, went away with feelings of antagonism towards it.

Instead of encouraging honest reflection and a willingness to question the validity of personal attitudes and beliefs (the aim of this book), the methods used on those early equal opportunities courses tended to confront and accuse.

Pause for thought

In Chapter 1 we suggested that if you weren't already, you should become a reflective thinker – *if you can't recall what we said about reflective thinking in that section why not take a few moments to re-read it now.* In order to develop your skills in this important area try a bit of reflective thinking now with the aid of the grid in Figure 4.1 and this pause for thought.

Just as it is wrong to stereotype members of minority groups by making judgements about who they are, based on only sketchy second-hand information, it's equally wrong to assume that members of majority groups (eg white people, able-bodied people, heterosexual people or men) spend all their time and energies engaged in acts of prejudice and discrimination.

Moreover, individuals may move from discrimination in one situation to non-discrimination in another and from conscious behaviour one moment to unconscious behaviour the next (see Figure 4.1).

- Look at the grid and identify the area which represents intentional discrimination. By intentional discrimination we mean knowingly doing something to the disadvantage of another person because you hold negative attitudes about them based on the fact that they are different from you. Try to think of any ways in which you have or might do this. If you are serious about getting to grips with treating others equally and fairly, you should strive to make this area of your behaviour as small as possible.
- The second area to scrutinize is the one labelled 'unintentional discrimination'. We probably all do this to one extent or another, and this book is peppered with examples of ways in which we might unintentionally discriminate against other people. Can you identify examples where you may have unintentionally discriminated against a member of a minority group?
- The third area is headed 'intentional non-discrimination' and this, along with the last area of the grid, are the two 'zones of non-discrimination' we want to encourage you to inhabit all of the time. Can you think of things you might have to change in order to operate in the intentional non-discrimination zone? By remaining aware of the ways in which discrimination and prejudice show themselves and by staying alert to our own capacity for such behaviour we intentionally try not to discriminate.
- The more you remain aware of your own negative attitudes towards others who are different from yourself and the way such attitudes influence your behaviour, the less conscious you will become of your non-discrimination. It will become so natural as to be an invisible part of you, ie: unintentional non-discrimination.

Sources of racism

The presence of racism in our society can be traced to a wide variety of sources.

Social structure

In some countries, racism has been part of the social structure and the law. Apartheid in South Africa and segregation in the Southern United States are just two examples. In Britain today, racism is illegal (see Chapter 10 for more details on UK legislation) but often its more subtle forms defy attempts to legislate for equal opportunities.

The legacy of slavery

The horror of slavery persisted in this country right up until the nineteenth century, with England playing one of the central roles in the trade in slaves throughout the colonized world. Its legacy of images of presumed white superiority cannot be ignored when we think about the roots of racism in this and indeed other countries.

Returning to institutional racism for a moment, it is important to note that little has been done in this country to acknowledge the part England played in slavery or to own it as a sad part of its real history. An illustration of this is how little focus slavery is given in the history taught in our own schools.

Pause for thought

Take a few moments to imagine a world in which this situation had been reversed and where slaves were white and slave-traders (considered the superior race, remember) black.

- What effects do you think this would have had on white culture in this country?
- If you think such a situation is inconceivable, try to examine how your own values have influenced your thinking on this issue.

The arrival of Commonwealth citizens

After the Second World War there was a great demand for labour arising from the need to undertake extensive rebuilding of war-damaged buildings, the fact that the British economy was growing and also as a result of the many men who had lost their lives fighting. Recruitment campaigns took place in several 'New Commonwealth' countries (particularly the Caribbean and the Indian sub-continent) during the 1950s leading to an increased settlement of Commonwealth citizens who had responded to the offer of work.

the UK was portrayed as a land of tolerance and opportunity

These recruitment campaigns portrayed the UK as a land of opportunity and tolerance where hard work was rewarded. Soon after their arrival on these shores, however, these new workers realized that the reality was to be very different.

> It was widely known throughout the West Indies that work was there for the taking. It was (much) less well known, however, that West Indians might expect to be demoted to a level below their skills or experience; they were normally used at a lower, and therefore cheaper, level of attainment and importance than they would have a right to expect in their homeland (Walvin, 1984: 108).

Resentment, fear and ignorance

There was also growing resentment and fear amongst the existing population, and overt acts of racism began to emerge. This fear and resentment had its basis in factors such as the following:

resentment and myths developed

- a view of black people as a threat to
  - British identity
  - jobs
  - housing
  - a white power-base
  - white culture;
- the fact that black people were not viewed as British although they held British passports and were part of the Commonwealth, and were helping rebuild a war-ravaged Britain; and
- popular myths whipped up by the media that Britain would become 'swamped by immigrants'.

Not only was the racism that flowed from this resentment direct and at times violent, it was also to become institutionalized through discriminatory housing and education policies.

In the 1950s there were disturbances in Notting Hill, London, where black people became victims of racial violence. To try to combat this, and to improve minority ethnic community relations in local areas of London, voluntary organizations were later set up which were originally called Community Relations Councils (CRCs). To clarify their role they are now known as Racial Equality Councils (RECs). They usually have a small professional staff of Racial Equality Officers (REOs), whose job it is to develop race relations within the community (see Chapter 10).

Personal racial prejudice

We noted above that one of the problems with anti-racist training was the aggressive way in which people were confronted with 'their racism' and how the very way it was done affected the way people felt both about the training and its subject. In noting this we are definitely not arguing that we don't all have an ongoing need to examine our attitudes. There are few of us who could claim that we have no prejudices against people whom we consider to be different from ourselves. What does need to be stressed is that it is not wrong in itself to discover prejudice in ourselves. The fact that we usually find this an uncomfortable experience is a natural process and a good sign – if it were not so, we might be tempted to conclude that we didn't care whether we held prejudices or not.

the approach of anti-racist training

In Chapter 1 we identified, in part, the nature of prejudice and how it involves an element of prejudgement on the part of the person holding it. This prejudgement is normally made before we have met the person as an individual and have found out much about them. It is probably true to say that nearly always, we change our opinion of a person after we have actually met them.

Think about times when you have had to join a new group which is made up of people whom you don't know – maybe when you attend a course, or start a new job, or when you go to college, or whatever. There you are looking around the group trying to decide what people are like: 'That person seems approachable', 'I like the way they dress', 'they seem my type', or 'he looks a nasty piece of work, I'll steer clear of him'. In other words you are forming first impressions, impressions based on only sketchy and patchy information. Having met them and having had the chance to get to know each of them better, the chances are that you will have to modify your initial impressions and the opinions they generated.

how do you make your decisions about people?

If you are white, the impressions you form about a black person you have not met before will most likely be influenced in part by their colour. There are many sources of images of black people that a white person receives. Where these are negative, they give rise to prejudice. The point is that these images can lock us into a 'cycle of subjectivity' (this is explained graphically in Figure 4.2). This simply means that as a rule, people tend to try to find evidence to support what they already believe rather than find evidence to contradict it.

negative images breed prejudice

The point can be illustrated by the general principle of law that a person is considered innocent until they are proven guilty. Prejudice on the other hand, tends to work in the opposite direction by declaring 'I will continue to hold my negative images and stereotypes until they are proved false'. Of course the dice are then well and truly loaded. All the subtle and obvious biases against black people which still exist in this country and which are threaded through our culture (and which we discuss in this chapter and in other parts of the book) fuel our negative imagery and it becomes harder and harder to break the cycle.

breaking the cycle of subjectivity

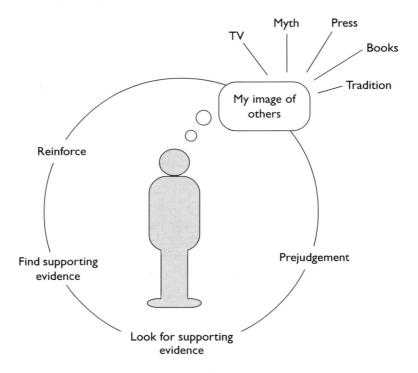

Figure 4.2   *The way we receive our images of other people sometimes locks us into a cycle of subjectivity which we may need to try to break out of*

One way to break out of the cycle described in Figure 4.2 is for us to follow the method that some researchers adopt and make a conscious effort to disprove our currently held attitudes and opinions. This will have the effect of making us stop looking for evidence to support negative images and instead make us start looking for things to *disprove* those negative images.

For example, imagine you're at a party chatting with a group of friends. At some point the conversation turns to the story of one of the group who has recently had their house broken into, to which someone says, 'probably black guys, most burglars are black, it's a well-known fact'. Instead of nodding and agreeing along with everyone else, why not . . .

- *Stop* for a second.
- *Think* about just how valid and true this assertion really is and how many assumptions it makes.
- *Resist* the temptation simply to justify these beliefs yourself. You may have examples that you could call upon that would support such racist assumptions as the one being voiced, but this is not at all surprising when

you consider that the main images we hold of black people in this country are still largely negative.

- *Reject* other people's prejudices rather than simply swallowing them and reinforcing them by nodding or saying nothing.
- *Respond* by disagreeing or by questioning what's been said. As we said immediately above, just saying nothing makes it seem as though you are giving tacit agreement and approval to what's been said – unfair but true!
- *Break out* of the cycle.
- *Break free* of racist assumptions.

Pause for thought

- Think about the images of black people presented in television advertising and in the newspapers.
- How do these images differ from the way that white people (in general) are depicted?
- What jobs or roles do black people typically get shown promoting on TV in programmes and adverts?
- Would you say that the images are becoming more positive or less?

Institutional racial prejudice

The reins of power in this country have for centuries been held by white males who have made official policy and determined how things should be, It is only recently (and only gradually) that we have begun to see black people reaching positions of political power. We have a very long way to go before we have a system that can represent the truly rich variety of cultures which go to make up modern Britain.

At the time of writing there are only five black MPs in the ruling Labour Party, a party that holds 416 seats in all. This represents about 1 per cent of all Labour MPs; a wholly unrepresentative figure considering that 5.5 per cent of the population are shown (by official statistics) as belonging to an ethnic minority group. Such figures show just how much work there is still to do if black people are to rise to positions of power. The situation is equally bad within institutions such as the legal profession with very few black judges.

black people are under-represented in political power

As we said in the opening chapters, the use of political power is often directed at maintaining the status quo (how things are) and at keeping those in power, in power. It was inevitable, therefore, that our institutions should develop in ways which proved disadvantageous to members of the black community. When parts of the social system discriminate against sections of the community we use the term institutional racism, ie racism that has become built into the ways in which we organize our society.

Following the outcome of the public inquiry in 1999 which investigated the murder of the young black student Stephen Lawrence, the whole issue of institutional discrimination in general and institutional racism in particular has become a crucial issue. The report that emerged from this inquiry threw up fundamental questions about the way our large institutions such as the police and the criminal justice system are arranged, and how they operate in ways which tend to discriminate against ethnic minority individuals and groups. In fact, the whole question of institutional discrimination holds important lessons for all of our major institutions including, health, housing, education and social services. Chapter 8 looks specifically at this issue.

The Stephen Lawrence inquiry

The Commission for Racial Equality (CRE) was set up in 1976 to enforce the race relations legislation in this country and to help promote equality of opportunity and good relations between people of different ethnic groups. Particular areas of its concern are employment, housing, education, and the provision of goods and services. All the evidence suggests that the CRE has a great deal of work still to do, not because of its own lack of effort but because of the mountain which is yet to be climbed. The CRE has a particular interest in discrimination on the grounds of a person's colour, race, nationality, or ethnic or national origins.

Commission for Racial Equality

Employment

The 1997–98 official government unemployment statistics summarised in Table 4.1 reveal several areas of inequality:

- Black Britons are up to three times more likely to be unemployed than their white counterparts. Young black men between the ages of 16–24 have an unemployment rate of 39 per cent.
- Those members of minority ethnic communities who are in work tend to have jobs with lower pay and lower status than white workers.
- Members of the black community experience far longer periods of unemployment between jobs than white people.

Pause for thought

- Think about the types of job that members of the black community typically have in this country. Do they tend to be similar, better or worse than those held by white people?

Being white

You might at first think that this is a strange title for this section. The thing is that many white people never stop for a moment and think about what their whiteness means. Because the majority of people in this country are white, whiteness tends to be assumed, and that assumption leads to the

whiteness is often assumed

Table 4.1 *Unemployment rates in the UK, 1997–98 (per cent)*

Ethnicity	Unemployed (%) by gender	
	Male	Female
White	9	6
Black	25	21
Indian	13	11
Pakistani/Bangladeshi	26	25
Chinese/Others	17	11

Source: Labour Force Survey, Office for National Statistics, 1999

acceptance that white is normal and anything else is in some way other than normal. If a person is unaware of their colour the chances are that they do not experience discrimination on the basis of it.

If you are not black, imagine how a person who *is* might feel. Brought up in a culture where most of the people and institutions assume whiteness, you are not only constantly reminded that you are black (and thus different) but you also face narrower opportunities as a result in terms of education, housing and employment. Do you think you would view the world in the same way as if your opportunities had been equal with those of everyone else?

Pause for thought

Look at the two lists below.

- Which list is most closely associated with black and which with white?
- Which list suggests negative images and which positive images?
- Can you think of other words to add to either list from your own experience?

death and mourning	birth and new life
evil	goodness
sin	purity
bad magic	good magic
extortion	lies which are not considered bad
the devil	God

RACIST MYTHOLOGY

There are many myths generated by racist thinking. The last part of this section considers some of the more common ones and tries to expose some of the many inconsistencies contained within each.

Myth

'I freely admit I'm a racist, I was born that way.'

Myth-buster

- There is no evidence to suggest that anyone is born with a particular attitude. Attitudes and opinions, just like culture, are *learnt,* so that one cannot be born a racist, and racism or racialism is not an hereditary trait of human behaviour. Racism flows out of learnt attitudes and behaviour, which are then reinforced by the stereotypes we choose to adopt.

  Think about how you voted at the last election (or if you were not old enough to vote, how you will vote in the next one). Do you think you were born Conservative or Labour, or Liberal Democrat, or did those opinions grow in you over a number of years? When you vote, you are not exercising any inborn tendency, but your own choice based on the things which have influenced you over the years.

  This aspect of choice is important. We choose to adopt a racist stance, no one forces us to. By the same token we can choose to embrace an anti-racist stance, ie against racism.

- Even if a person could genuinely (but wrongly) believe themselves to have been born a racist, any such behaviour would be subject to the law. In Chapter 10 we discuss the laws in this country which are designed to promote equality of opportunity, as well as those which are designed to control behaviour – for instance, incitement to racial hatred is a criminal offence under the Public Order Act 1986, for which you can be sent to prison!

- Think for a moment of all the influences there have been on you, as you have developed into the person you are today. Figure 4.3 shows some of those that we can think of. All these and many more have gone to socialize you into the person you are.

Myth

'There is little, if any, racism in this country – it's all hype!'

Myth-buster

There is ample evidence that racism exists in the United Kingdom. One way of knowing this is the number of cases which still need to be brought by the Commission for Racial Equality on behalf of victims of racial prejudice. Another is the number of racist attacks reported by members of minority ethnic communities.

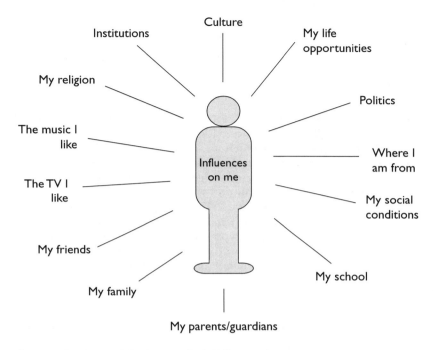

Figure 4.3   *Some of the factors which influence the way we are*

Parliament has passed laws to try to ensure that all citizens are treated equally, and to eliminate racism and racist behaviour from Britain, Although some progress has been made, there are still many signs of disadvantage. Just one illustration of this is the number of requests for help received by the Commission for Racial Equality. In 1992, for example, the CRE received 1,557 requests for assistance, in 1998 this number had risen to 10,000 specific requests for help from individuals who felt they had been the victims of racism.

continuing evidence of disadvantage and discrimination

In a social attitudes survey published in 1992, people were asked whether they felt there was more or less prejudice than there had been five years previously:

- 24 per cent thought there was more;
- 24 per cent thought there was less;
- 50 per cent thought it was about the same.

Source: Jowell *et al*, 1992

Myth

'Minority ethnic groups are racist themselves, they keep their culture and language and make no attempt to integrate into our culture.'

Myth-buster

- Racism, in its strictest sense, is about the use of *power* by the majority or the controlling group (normally they are one and the same) in order to keep another group both weak and at a disadvantage.
- What does 'our culture' mean? Look at Chapter 3 again and think about how diverse British culture really is. Who has the right to say that they have the monopoly on British culture?
- The statement begs the question, 'How easy does the majority group make it for other groups to join in without losing their identity?' Our society still needs laws to prevent discrimination; are we really surprised that people find it difficult to integrate?
- Britain is a multi-cultural society and all the richer for it! That is a reality and will not change.

Myth

'They should go back to where they came from.'

Myth-buster

- The fact is that at least 50 per cent of those with a Caribbean background and 30 per cent of those with an Asian background were born in this country, and this figure is of course rising, so these people *are* where they came from.
- If you agreed with the statement above, how many generations would you include? Would you also include the Scots, Welsh and Irish?
- If all those who can trace their roots to settlement to these shores were to leave, the fabric of our society would collapse.
- During most of the post-war period there was a net outflow of people from the UK, ie more people left than arrived.
- On the very day this was written we heard a radio interview with a black woman who had emigrated with her husband to Jamaica. Both she and her husband had been born in this country, and both were absolutely fed up with being asked where they were from. She reported that even at school her teachers asked her the question. 'How can you possibly feel British', she said, 'if everybody assumes that you are not?'

Myth

'Britain should be kept for the British.'

Myth-buster

The problem underlying this myth is that it fails to address the question of who do we mean by 'the British'? Does the term exclude all those whose roots are not in the soil we call Britain, and yet who have British nationality? If so, a ridiculous list of people who would be excluded is generated. Poles, Ukrainians, Italians, Cypriots, Turks, New Zealanders, Australians, Afro-Caribbeans, Asians, South Asians, Americans, Iranians, Kurds, Greeks, Bangladeshis, Indians, Pakistanis . . .

Myth

'When in Rome do as the Romans do.'

Myth-buster

- This particular saying has its roots in the fourth century. St Augustine (as he later became) crossed the Mediterranean from North Africa to live in Milan. His mother Monica joined him there, and being a pious Christian woman was used to fasting on Saturdays (as was also the custom among the Roman Christians). The Milan Christians, however, did not follow this custom and Monica was uncertain what to do. She asked Augustine for advice and he, in turn, sought help from the bishop of Milan, St Ambrose. His advice was not to fast on Saturday in Milan but 'when in Rome do as the Romans do' (Poulter, 1986).

  When this old saying is advanced as a justification for discriminatory behaviour, it makes it sound as though the speaker has a monopoly on what constitutes the cultural practices of this country. The reality is that more often than not, the people against whom this argument is advanced *are* in their own country. Metaphorically they are in Rome, and they themselves are Romans!
- The way people often deal with the differences in culture is to play down the differences between their personal culture and others whom they consider to be in 'their' group, and amplify the differences they see in the culture of a person who has an ethnic background which is different to their own.
- So to insist that 'when in Rome, a person should do as the Romans do' reveals:
  - a false and narrow assumption about what is British culture;

- – an arrogant assumption that the speaker has the right to determine what another person's culture is, and should be; and
- – a 'them and us' way of thinking which only serves to make the
  divide between groups even deeper.
- To be British means to be a member of a multi-ethnic, multi-religious
  society. That is the way things are.

KEY POINTS IN THIS CHAPTER

In Chapter 4 we have:

- looked at how racial prejudices and discrimination arise;
- discussed the idea of race and noted that the word can be misleading as
  it has associations with outdated biological theories;
- considered the nature of racism, both personal and institutional, and
  had a brief look at its sources and effects;
- considered intentional and unintentional forms of racism and how they
  differ;
- examined the use of language and how inappropriate language can
  undermine fairness, sensitivity and equality;
- looked at employment as a measure of how there is still a long way to go
  to achieve equality in this country; and
- exploded some of the myths about racism which have developed.

PERSONAL ACTION PLAN

Try answering the following questions:

How will the things I have learnt in this chapter change the way I
think and act towards others who are different to me?

What has this chapter helped me to learn about myself with regard to:

- my beliefs;
- my attitudes;
- my values;
- my knowledge of others;
- my behaviour;
- my use of language;
- my responsibilities;
- the way I see the world?

How do I need to change in order to become:

- fairer;
- more sensitive;
- more understanding;
- less prejudicial;
- less discriminatory;
- better able to deal with people according to their needs?

If I were to change one thing about the way I act as a result of reading this chapter what would it be?

Chapter 5

Sexism

Some of the most deeply rooted of all fixed attitudes are those concerning the type of roles that women should fulfil and the positions that they should be allowed to hold in our society. This chapter will look at these attitudes and also at what consequences they have for women's chances of being treated fairly and equally. After you have finished reading this chapter we hope you will have a better understanding of:

- the terms 'sex', 'gender' and 'sexism';
- issues surrounding the changing role and status of women;
- some of the facts about women and employment;
- some of the ways in which discrimination against women operates; and
- ways in which women may be the subject of sexual harassment.

GENDER AND SEX DIFFERENCES

Pause for thought

- Imagine that an alien has landed from another planet and can speak your language! The alien, having no knowledge of the differences between men and women, asks you to explain how men and women are different. What would you say?
- Did you confine your answer to just biological differences? Don't forget other types of differences as well.
- If this visitor from space asked you why men and women tended to do different types of work in your society and to hold different positions of status and power, how would you explain these arrangements?

Gender

Whereas the word 'sex' (as in the phrase 'men and women are different sexes') refers to *anatomy* and the *biological* differences between men and women, 'gender', on the other hand, is used to mean the differences between men and women which are *psychological, cultural* or *social.* The strength of these 'gender' differences may vary depending on the society, but most people agree that by far the strongest influence on gender differences is the way that children are brought up and what they are taught about the world around them. This process is sometimes called socialization. Consider the following example:

Research done at various hospital maternity units looked at the way that relatives behaved when visiting parents and their new-born babies to see whether the sex of the baby made a difference to that behaviour. They found that when visiting male babies, relatives would often use heavily masculine words and phrases such as 'what a little buster' or 'he's a real bruiser'. With girls, they tended to use terms like 'isn't she sweet' or 'she's so gentle'. They would even handle the babies in different ways.

This suggests that gender is influenced right from birth and continues to be reinforced through childhood, adolescence and adulthood. In fact these gender differences are so noticeable, even at the nursery stage, that it's understandable how they have come to be seen by many people as natural and in-built.

gender refers to psychological, cultural and social differences

the process starts even with babies

The influence of television and books

A good example of how images of gender (of what boys and girls should be like) are reinforced can be seen in television commercials aimed at children. You only have to glance at these to realize the strength of gender stereotyping that the children are being subjected to.

Commercials aimed at young girls carry strong messages about gentleness and motherhood, with images of dolls being cuddled and with washing, ironing and housework to be done. Commercials aimed at young boys are very often macho, militaristic and powerful, or stress that boys should be interested in engineering, construction and science. Faced with such a bombardment, it is little wonder that boys tend to grow up mistakenly thinking they have a dominant role to play and that women should focus their efforts and skills on rearing children and looking after a home. It is these gender stereotypes (fixed ways of looking at what men and women should be like) which underpin sexism (treating women less favourably than men because of their gender).

television, books and stories all influence gender

The images portrayed in books and stories are also known to have a powerful influence on the way ideas about gender are learnt. Although now dated, research by Lenore Weitzman and others in 1972 (reported in Giddens, 1989) showed that in the most widely used pre-school books there were clear differences in the gender roles of the characters portrayed. In summary, they found that in these schoolbooks:

- Males played a larger part in the stories and pictures than females.
- Girls in the stories were shown as passive and confined to indoor activities;

boys, on the other hand, were shown as active, adventurous and mainly engaged in outdoor activities.

- Of the adults represented in the stories, any women who were not wives or mothers were witches or fairy godmothers (effectively not real people).
- Men were depicted as fighters, kings, judges and police officers.

Pause for thought

- Think about the stories *you* were exposed to as a child, including familiar fairy stories. Do you think you were influenced in any way by the way males and females were depicted?
- Do you think we should be providing young children with books that show more balanced pictures of female roles and expectations? If so, why?

Sexism

Defined in its simplest form, sexism is the unfair or unequal treatment of women by men. Sexism is unique among most other forms of discrimination in that its victims do not belong to a minority group. Of the resident population of Great Britain in 1998,

there are more women than men in Britain

- 51 per cent were women (29,165,000)
- 49 per cent were men (28,169,000)
  Source: Population Trends; Winter 1998. Office for National Statistics

Reinforcing gender differences, and *making them matter* either at the personal level, or by institutions or even society, is what gives rise to sexism.

Sex Discrimination Act 1975

The Sex Discrimination Act 1975, is one piece of legislation which was designed to combat prejudice based on gender. Although prejudice against a person based on their gender is recognized by this law as being a two-way process (ie a man can also claim discrimination on the basis of his gender), in our society today the *real* issue is the unequal treatment of women. As you go through the chapter you will see that most of the power over life opportunities in this country is held by men. Although there has been a considerable change in attitudes towards equality over recent years, there is still a huge inequality gap between the opportunities enjoyed by men and those enjoyed by women.

there is still a huge inequality gap in this country

THE CHANGING ROLE AND STATUS OF WOMEN

Male domination

Although different cultures around the world do have differences in the types of work performed by men and women and the positions they are allowed to hold in their communities, there is no known society where females are generally more powerful than men. This is the case even though there is absolutely no evidence to suggest that there is a genetic difference in the intellectual ability of women, or that differences in physical strength can account for why men should be dominant.

male domination is a worldwide phenomenon

Men, although they are the minority group, still outnumber women in all spheres of power and influence, and it is against this background that we need to view the problems of discrimination against women. Historically, women have been disadvantaged and have been moulded into certain roles and expectations and subject to greater limitations and far narrower opportunities than men.

Pause for thought

- How do you account for the fact that almost universally, males have dominant roles?
- How could this be changed?

We have said in earlier chapters that the group that holds the power to make the rules and to direct social arrangements will create some of those rules and popularize certain ways of thinking and behaving amongst members of the community in order to protect their own hold on power. This ensures that they won't have their authority challenged by others. Our society is dominated by men, so it is hardly surprising that many of these arrangements keep things as they are, with men in charge.

'he' who holds the power makes the rules

Increasingly, rules and arrangements which favour men and discriminate against women are being challenged, as are dominant attitudes that men are the wage-earners and the ones best suited to fill the higher positions in government and industry. For instance, the 'biological justification' which states that, as women are the only ones who can have children, they are naturally intended to fulfil the role of child-rearer and primary carer is being questioned. It could easily be argued that once the mother has done her 'biological bit' (including breast-feeding if this is what she chooses) there is no reason why men should not then take over the care of infants and young children. The fact that this seems such an unusual and, some might say, laughable arrangement, is good evidence of just how deeply rooted our attitudes about gender and the roles men and women should perform actually are.

Political power and the right to vote

If we were using exceptions to prove a rule then it would be fairly easy to identify many exceptional women from the last century who wielded considerable political power: Indira Gandhi of India, Golda Meir of Israel, Benazir Bhutto of Pakistan and Margaret Thatcher of the UK, to name just four. But the achievements of these individuals, remarkable as they are, mask a considerable imbalance in the numbers of women who have political power. In the closing year of the last century, there were five female Cabinet members out of 22.

the exceptions of powerful women do not prove the rule

Things seem to be changing very slowly in the political arena, and even after the election of the New Labour administration in 1997 the number of women involved in government or opposition remains proportionately low. In 1999 about 18 per cent of all MPs were women (*source*: *House of Commons Weekly Information Bulletin*, August 1999). The European scene was only marginally better with 21 per cent of the British members of the European Parliament being women (*source*: *The Guardian*, 15 June 1999). Why this should be is still largely a matter of speculation, although it is quite likely that the factors which make it so hard for women to rise to the top levels of industry and commerce operate with even more vigour in politics. These include:

- The enormous drain on an individual's time if they are to rise to the key political positions. Far fewer women, particularly if they choose to have children (and then become locked into a childcare role), are able to devote the time it takes to reach the top positions.
- The alleged operation of the 'old boys' network in selection for key positions. Even where the policy is one of promotion to key jobs on merit alone, there are far fewer suitably qualified women (in terms of experience) to choose from. This is largely because access to such suitably qualified previous positions is not there for them in the first place.
- Men also set the very standards by which women will be judged when they apply for senior positions, and these may discriminate against women because they are based on male assumptions of a 'woman's place'.
- Political power might well represent the ultimate in the ability to influence things in this country. Are men especially reluctant to loosen their grip on this?

The right to vote

Women's involvement in the political life of this country has not, of course, had nearly so long to evolve as has been the case for men. Even though the fight for the right of women to vote on a fair and equal basis with men had caused great conflict and hardship for the leaders of the women's movement, at the first national election in 1929 (when women were first entitled to

equal rights to vote did not come until 1929

vote on an equal basis with men) only about one-third of those eligible did so. This situation has now changed and, in the past 20 years, the difference between the numbers of men and women voting has not been significant.

Much of the social and political change which has taken place over the last hundred years has been influenced by the various feminist movements. A feminist (who, incidentally, might be a woman or a man) is simply a person who strives for equality under the law between women and men, and for the upgrading of legislation as it becomes outdated.

feminists

A key event in the evolution of feminist movements in this country was when, in 1866, a petition signed by 1,500 women was presented to Parliament. It demanded full voting rights for women. Having been largely ignored, the organizers of the petition founded the National Society for Women's Suffrage (suffrage is another word for 'vote'). Active supporters of the movement became known as 'suffragettes', one of their leaders being Emmeline Pankhurst. Figure 5.1 shows some of the key events in the growth of rights for women, which owes much to the work of the early campaigners.

Childcare and housework

Childcare

There is little doubt that many, if not most, of the problems of inequality for women stem from perceptions that the primary role of women is to have and care for children. Whereas for most men the main life choice is their career, for most women, society expects that marriage and children should be their main concern.

'So great is the presumption that women's primary role is to bear children . . . that women are still asked at interviews if they have families or family obligations, a question rarely asked of men' (Calvert and Calvert, 1992: 7).

'Males tend to dominate the higher levels because simply [*sic*] the women drop out to have babies and that sort of thing' (a top male manager, quoted in Homans, 1987: 85).

Pause for thought

- How has society changed in terms of the way it sees the roles of men and women in your lifetime?
- How has this affected what is considered to be the proper role of women and men?

	1900	1950	1990
RIGHT TO VOTE AND PARTICIPATE IN DEMOCRATIC GOVERNMENT	1893 Vote for and representation on county councils 1918 Parliamentary elections if 25 (only 21 for men) 1919 Women may be MPs (Lady Astor) 1923 First woman cabinet minister (Margaret Bondfield) 1928 Fully equal voting rights		1979 First woman PM (Margaret Thatcher) 1990 Fewer women MPs than at any time since 1929
RIGHTS TO OWN PROPERTY	1882 Married Women's Property Act (changed law whereby a woman's property ceased to be her own on marriage)		1990 Right to separate taxation regardless of amount of income
RIGHT OF EQUAL ACCESS TO JOBS	1919 Right of entry to the professions established		1975 Formal discrimination against women in most other occupations abolished
RIGHT TO EQUAL PAY FOR EQUAL WORK		1946 Royal Commission recommended equal pay in teaching, local government and civil service	1970 Equal Pay Act 1975 Sex Discrimination Act (intended to establish the principle of equal pay for equal work)

Figure 5.1 *Some of the key features in the development of rights for women*

Some of the changes you identified might have included:

- Attitudes towards birth control, which is increasingly being seen as the responsibility of both partners.
- More women are choosing not to have children.
- A greater acceptance of child-minders, day nurseries and crèche facilities.
- Higher levels of male unemployment have meant that some women have become the main wage-earners.
- Smaller families, which reduce the time commitment needed to rear children.
- Economic expansion, especially during the 1980s increased the amount of work available. (However, this has contracted again in the 1990s and, as we will see below, the type of work done by women tends to be lower-paid and often part-time, which still gives rise to enormous inequality.)

The family

Traditional family patterns are still changing. Of the people of working age with dependent children, 680,000 (90 per cent) are lone parent women compared with 79,000 (10 per cent) lone parent men (*source*: EOC Analysis of the Labour Force Survey, Spring 1998, Office for National Statistics).

These figures show that the role of women in the family is no longer the one traditionally assumed; namely that of mother and home-maker who devotes her time to caring for and rearing children, looking after the household and offering support to her husband. While this is still the pattern which many choose to adopt, over three-quarters of a million women have to bring up children *and* earn an income alone. It is no longer sufficient to define women's role in society solely in terms of childbearing and home-making.

traditional family patterns are still changing

Housework

In pre-industrial times there was much less division between so-called housework and paid employment. Providing for the needs of the family was the concern of both parents, and this can still be seen in non-industrial Third World countries. Since the Industrial Revolution, the roles of wage-earner and home-maker have become separated, with home-making and caring for children being seen generally as the responsibility of women, and earning a wage (or being the 'breadwinner') as the responsibility of the man in the household.

housework became a primary role for women

The possibilities for overturning these fixed attitudes about what roles men and women should fulfil were amply illustrated in both world wars, most notably in the second, where women were actively encouraged to leave the home to take the place of the men. By successfully working on the land, in the armed forces, in industry and other occupations which supported

women's
involvement
in the war
showed there
could be a
different way

the war effort, women demonstrated that the traditional barriers to their involvement in the economic life of the nation could be broken down.

On the return of men from the war, however, propaganda through the media, especially women's magazines, again encouraged women to stay at home to support and cater for their men. Indeed women, from being promoted as heroines of the war effort, once again became the housekeepers and some, who wanted to stay on in work, even faced intolerable hostility from workers in factories who considered that they were keeping hold of jobs which should be given to fathers who needed to provide for their families.

Housework is still seen mainly as the responsibility of women, even where the woman is also working full time in paid employment. The British Social Attitudes Survey (Jowell, *et al* 1992) reveals some of the attitudes towards domestic responsibilities.

In response to the statement: 'A husband's job is to earn the money, a wife's job is to look after the home and family', 41 per cent of male respondents and 47 per cent of female respondents disagreed or strongly disagreed (interestingly, only about a third of men and women agreed). On the face of it, then, we might say that a significant proportion of the population rejects the traditional model of women being home-makers and men being the breadwinners.

Answering a different question however – one about what *actually happens in the home,* the answers show a different story (see Jowell, *et al* 1992). In response to the question: 'Who is responsible for general domestic duties?', the percentage of respondents (those people who answered the questionnaire) who said it was mainly the woman's responsibility were as follows:

- in households where both the man and woman work full time: 67 per cent,
- in households where the man works full time and the woman part time: 83 per cent, and
- in households where the man works full time and the woman is not in paid employment: 89 per cent.

Clearly, although a significant number of people might say that they don't support the idea that a woman's place is in the home, the practice is very different.

Employment and status

The pursuit of equality in employment is firmly rooted in two treaties to which Britain has signed up, and also in its own equal opportunities legislation.

- Britain, in joining the EEC in 1973, subscribed, amongst others, to Article 119 of the Treaty of Rome which requires member states to maintain the principles of equal pay for equal work regardless of gender.
- This is also enshrined in the United Nations Universal Declaration of Human Rights, article 23(2): 'Everyone, without any discrimination, has the right to equal pay for equal work'.

Despite the legislation to redress the balance, men's earnings and occupational status in society are still considerably greater than women's, and their overall dominance in society remains. Although women have equal rights to all but a very few occupations, they continue to be over-represented in both low-paid and part-time work and under-represented in the professions.

Many of the sources of discrimination are still visible today. Women are very under-represented among other areas – in politics, the judiciary, and the church, for example – and it is particularly in the area of employment that the effects of discrimination against women in society are well illustrated.

Part-time work

Most part-time work in this country is done by women. In 1998, 83 per cent of all part-time employees were female (*source*: Labour Force Survey, Spring 1998, Office for National Statistics). Part-time working has traditionally been associated with lower-paid, unskilled or semi-skilled work and is much less secure, often failing to attract benefits available to full-time workers.

We do need to take care not to paint an entirely negative picture. Many organizations have introduced the opportunity to continue to pursue careers whilst job-sharing or working part-time, so we need to recognize that the part-time labour force will contain an element of those who are actually taking advantage of arrangements to help them continue their careers. Others choose part-time work simply because it suits them or they wish to pursue other interests.

The incidence of part-time work also seems to be related to family circumstances. Female employees who have one or more dependent children are almost twice as likely to work part-time as those who do not have a dependent child. This situation seems to raise several issues about the equal opportunities and life chances of women.

- The overwhelming evidence is that women still have the responsibility for dealing with children, although there have been considerable changes in the definition of what constitutes a family group.
- Generally speaking this responsibility for children means that they are restricted to not working, taking part-time work which is usually of lower status (as viewed by society) and which offers lower pay, or taking work where the hours and holidays fit in with those of school term times and holidays. Many people are put off even considering advancement to

Treaty of Rome

Universal Declaration of Human Rights

despite equal rights women are still under-represented in the best jobs

most part-time work is done by women

responsibility for children makes a huge difference to the life chances of women

managerial positions because many employers do not allow their senior staff to work part-time.
- Until there are better arrangements for the provision of childcare facilities for those who want them, and a change in the attitude of some employers to recognise that opportunities need to be given to all, ie for men and women, to combine being carers with a career, the situation is unlikely to improve.

Pause for thought

- If we are right in assuming that a significant proportion of those working part-time do not do so by choice, but by force of circumstances; what would need to change to give those people equal opportunities with others?

Low pay

Some facts about low pay:

- The majority of workers who fall below the low-pay threshold are female.
- In most manual and some non-manual occupations, the average hourly earnings of female full-time employees falls below the low-pay threshold.
- In almost all manual occupations, the average hourly earnings of female part-timers falls below the low-pay threshold.

Pay of managers and professionals

earnings of managers and professionals are still not equal

Across all the professions there is an imbalance in pay in favour of men. There is an imbalance across the professions generally but this is most marked in the pay of managers. The Equal Opportunities Commission (EOC) pay briefing for January 1997 noted that at the rate of progress being made at the time women would have to wait until 2040 to get equal pay across the board. In 1997 the gap in pay between men and women employed by banks and building societies was reported to be 36 per cent. Women in professional and managerial positions earned only 80–90 per cent of their male counterparts' pay (*source*: EOC Pay Briefing, 1997, *EOC online information*). This is despite the existence of equal pay legislation.

Representation of women in occupational groups

There are considerable differences in the way women are represented in the various occupation groups. Figure 5.2 illustrates some areas which give revealing insights into the way women are represented. It is worth considering what the causes of the differences may be.

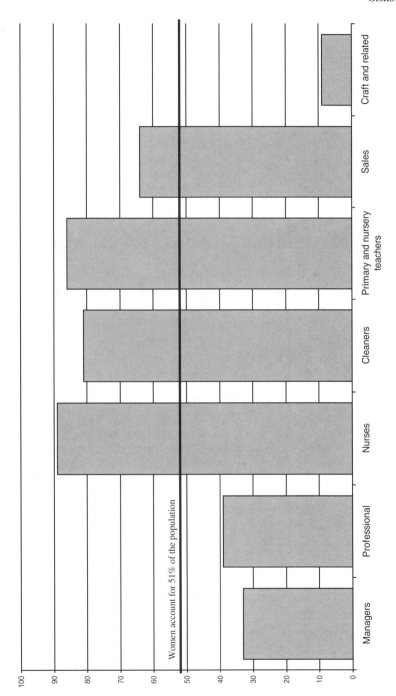

Figure 5.2 *Female share of employment – percentage of selected occupation groups*
Source: The EOC analysis of the Labour Force Survey, Spring 1998. Office for National Statistics.

Pause for thought

We have noted in this section that women are over-represented in part-time work and occupations attracting low pay, and under-represented in careers which attract higher pay. Before you leave this chapter consider the organization in which you work (or perhaps used to work).

• How much are women represented in that organization?
• How many of them are in key positions with power?
• Is the culture of the organization male-dominated?
• Is there anything which *you* could do to help redress any imbalance you might identify?

OTHER FORMS OF DISCRIMINATION AGAINST WOMEN

In this chapter so far, we have identified many ways in which it is quite obvious that women are the subject of discrimination. Other forms of discrimination and prejudice, however, are much more subtle.

Sexist language

We have already noted the power of language as a factor in discrimination in Chapter 2. Some examples relating to sexism include:

• Name-calling in derogatory terms – this has the effect of putting a woman down.
• Language which effectively fails to recognize the contribution of women. For example, using as a general term 'policemen' rather than police officer, or 'fireman' rather than fire-fighter (this is often called 'exclusionary language').
• Referring in general terms to senior personnel in the male gender, 'he', 'his' and so on, as if there were no female senior personnel nor could there be.

Myth

'Why should I worry about what I say? Things have gone to ridiculous lengths. I'm not going to be one of the "politically correct brigade".'

Myth-buster

Such people will quite likely object to the use of the word chair instead of chairman and so on. The argument is generally that such language is unnecessary and trivial. Such an approach, however, prompts the following questions:

- If the required changes in language are so trivial, why not accept them?
- How far does the old terminology reinforce bad stereotypes?
- How much power over women does the objector stand to lose?
- What is the effect, for example, of constantly referring to adult females as 'girls' in circumstances where boys are not referred to as 'boys', but as 'men'?

Sexual harassment

Sexual harassment is usually defined as being repeated and unwanted verbal or sexual advances. The Equal Opportunities Commission, Trades Union Congress and Department of Employment all identify sexual harassment, particularly at work, as a problem which continues to give rise to concern. While there can be a sexually explicit component in sexual harassment of women by men, another, perhaps stronger, motivation may be men reinforcing their power over women, and reminding women of their vulnerability. In such circumstances such behaviour may have little, if any, sexual motivation.

sexual harassment is an ongoing problem

Sexual harassment often has two distinct but key elements, in that it is behaviour which is usually persistent and unwanted. The following are examples of behaviour towards women which is clearly unacceptable and will often amount to sexual harassment:

behaviour which amounts to sexual harassment

- Requests for sexual favours – for example, hints that sexual favours will advance a career, or retard it if they are not given. This is often made worse because, as we have seen above in the section on women and employment, women frequently find themselves at a disadvantage in the power structure, as in the case where a male boss sexually harasses his female secretary. She may find herself relatively powerless to do anything about it.
- Wolf-whistles, or unsolicited verbal remarks of a sexual nature. These include degrading comments like 'look at the legs (and other parts of a woman's anatomy) on that', and 'hello gorgeous'. Such comments emphasize women as sex objects while reinforcing power over them – some men assume they have the right to make such comments. At the same time this type of behaviour can influence a woman's view of herself, making it difficult for her to see herself as a fully functioning and effective professional. The net result is that women subjected to such harassment have to work harder to get themselves taken seriously.
- Uninvited physical contact.

- Displaying or circulating sexually suggestive material. Sexual harassment sometimes occurs in the form of nude pin-ups, calendars and the like in offices, canteens, shop-floors and so on.
- Unwanted sexual advances. Where 'no' is not taken for an answer.
- Insults or ridicule because of one's gender.
- Anything which interferes with the individual's performance or creates an intimidating, hostile or offensive environment.

Sexual harassment and equal opportunities legislation

Sexual harassment is not specifically defined in the Sex Discrimination Act 1975. The most serious forms of harassment may amount to a serious criminal offence, but behaviour which does not amount to a criminal offence may nevertheless give rise to a complaint under the Sex Discrimination Act.

sexual harassment can be dealt with under the Sex Discrimination Act 1975

In 1985 the Scottish Court of Appeal ruled, in the case of *Porcelli* v. *Strathclyde Regional Council*, that a woman who had complained of sexual harassment had been the victim of unlawful sex discrimination. The facts of the case were that a woman was resented by two male colleagues who tried to make her apply for a transfer to another post by being vindictive and unpleasant towards her. Their tactics included personal insults, obscene language, intimidation and brushing up against her.

Since her successful claim, there have been many other cases of sexual harassment ranging from the minor to the more serious. It is worth noting that employers are not only responsible for their own conduct towards employees, but are also liable for discriminatory acts committed by their employees, if that behaviour occurs at work. So whether you are an employer, employee or someone responsible for others at work, it is worth remembering that this is a problem which involves you.

KEY POINTS IN THIS CHAPTER

- We identified the meaning of the terms 'sex', 'gender' and 'sexism', and noted that we believe gender differences to be heavily influenced by the way children are brought up and taught about the world around them.
- We considered the changing role and status of women in this country and identified ways in which the traditional ideas of what constitutes a family are changing in that many women have an expanded role of carer and wage-earner.
- We also took a look at the issues of employment and pay, as these give a good indicator of just how much there is still to do if true equality is to become a reality.
- We examined the part that housework plays in sexism and how common assumptions about which roles and responsibilities belong to which gender further undermine women's access to equal opportunities.

- We identified one of the chief factors in inequality between women and men, namely the common assumption that a woman's primary role is to bear children and care for them.
- We noted that discrimination against women can take the form of sexual harassment. Women should not have to put up with such treatment and the Sex Discrimination Act and criminal law are there to offer protection.

PERSONAL ACTION PLAN

Try answering the following questions:

How will the things I have learnt in this chapter change the way I think and act towards others who are different to me?

What has this chapter helped me to learn about myself with regard to:

- my beliefs;
- my attitudes;
- my values;
- my knowledge of others;
- my behaviour;
- my use of language;
- my responsibilities;
- the way I see the world?

How do I need to change in order to become:

- fairer;
- more sensitive;
- more understanding;
- less prejudicial;
- less discriminatory;
- better able to deal with people according to their needs?

If I were to change one thing about the way I act as a result of reading this chapter what would it be?

Chapter 6

Sexuality

We are going to look at many of the issues surrounding sexuality and fair treatment in an honest, open and straightforward way. Throughout the chapter we will be asking you questions and raising issues which we hope will get you thinking about how you, others and society in general think about and behave towards gay men and lesbians. After you've read it through you should have a better understanding of the following:

- the images we may hold of gay men and lesbians and where these images come from;
- how these images and stereotypes can strengthen prejudice and isolate gay men and lesbians;
- the importance of understanding clothing and lifestyle;
- gay and lesbian relationships;
- the types of inequality gay men and lesbians experience; and
- direct forms of prejudice and discrimination against gay men and lesbians.

INTRODUCTION

The more strongly you disagree with the values and sexual way of life of people who are different from you in some way, the more likely it is that you will hold negative views about them. At the same time, the more strongly negative you feel about them and what you believe they stand for, the more intolerant you are likely to be towards that person or group of persons.

In our experience, the extension of fair treatment and equal opportunities towards gay men and lesbians can and does generate such extreme attitudes, and in turn these negative attitudes keep a whole series of stereotypes and myths alive. Let's be honest from the outset, this is an emotive area and one where many people feel unable or unwilling to question the beliefs that they hold.

But fair treatment and equal opportunities *cannot and must not* be restricted only to certain groups and individuals on the basis that it's just too challenging to extend them to everyone. If this were to be the case they would no longer be *fair* treatment or *equal* opportunities in the truest and widest sense. Remember, you cannot 'bolt down' prejudices and hope they will remain hidden, because sooner or later they will escape and they will

sexuality is an emotive issue

fair treatment is for all

influence your behaviour. If you have a genuine desire to be fair and to treat people equally this must include *everyone*.

Pause for thought

Before moving on, it's very important that you should try and take stock of where you stand on these issues.

- Think about the terms gay man and lesbian and write down some of the images that these words create for you.
- Where have these images and ideas come from?
- How many of the ideas and images you hold of gay men and lesbians arise out of your own direct experience?
- How many of the things you have written down are negative and how many positive?

THE IMAGES WE HOLD

Let's lay to rest two commonly held views about gay men and lesbians, views which are thankfully becoming less accepted and acceptable.

Myth

'Gay men and lesbians are suffering from a type of illness which prevents them from adopting a healthy sexual orientation.'

Myth-buster

There is no scientific evidence that supports the view that the sexual orientation of gay men and lesbians is a form of illness. Remember too that such views have consequences both for the person who holds them and for the person towards whom they are directed. Thinking of gay and lesbian sexual orientation as an illness requires that you view gay men and lesbians as ill and in need of medical treatment. But by dealing with them on this basis you would be acting in ways which they themselves would wholly reject as in any way fair and which they would find deeply offensive.

This statement is full of beliefs about what is normal and natural sexuality. Having read previous chapters, you will realize that views and beliefs about what is to be considered normal and natural are *constructed* by the majority group and because of this are *relative* ideas about others rather than fixed truths. Because these views and ideas about what should be considered normal and natural have been passed down over generations without being questioned, we often take them as fact, just as once people firmly believed that the earth was flat.

ideas of 'normal' come from many sources

These ideas about what constitutes normal (and indeed abnormal) sexuality, and about what gay and lesbian might mean, come from many different sources that may include the following:

- our family and friends;
- television;
- magazines;
- newspapers;
- films;
- radio;
- advertising;
- teachers; and
- direct experience.

Of course members of our family, our friends and other people who may hold influence over us have had their own views about sexuality shaped and influenced through a process of upbringing and education and through exposure to media images and messages, just as we have. This is how group meanings are transmitted and how group ideas and prejudices are kept alive (see Figure 6.1). But by becoming aware of how your own views and ideas are shaped by and grow out of the attitudes and values of others, you will be in a better position to ask just how valid such beliefs and opinions are for *you* and how compatible they are to the principles of equality and fair treatment.

Myth

'Gay men and lesbians are deviants who have chosen this particular lifestyle knowing it is wrong.'

Myth-buster

Such a view talks about *deviant* behaviour but it often doesn't say *from what* the behaviour is supposed to deviate. The answer is, as we have said above, that it deviates from the majority view of what is normal. It also uses the word 'wrong' as if ideas of right and wrong are obvious, absolute and fixed rather than flexible, relative and changing.

Let's look at a couple of well-known examples of how ideas of right and wrong are flexible and relative rather than always fixed and self-apparent.

- During the 1920s in certain states of America it was considered wrong to drink alcohol – this was the time of the so-called 'prohibition'. Some years later the laws barring the sale and drinking of

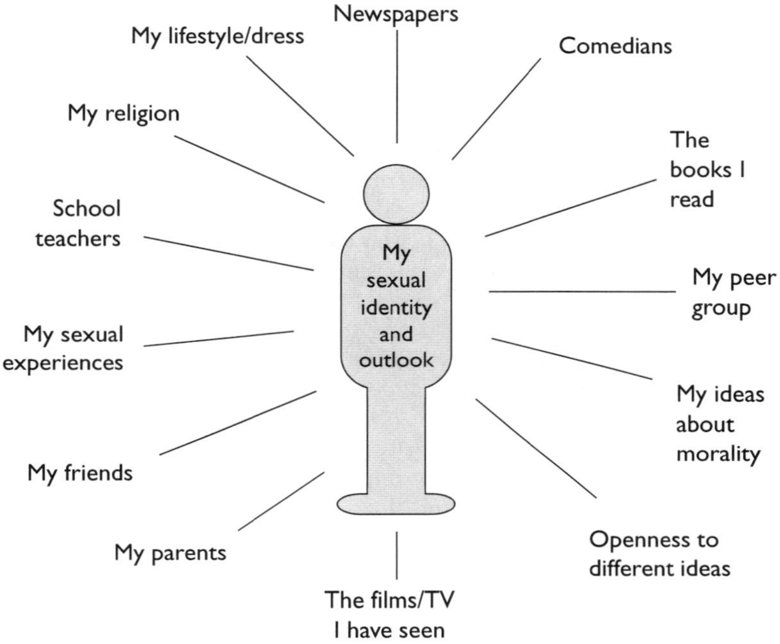

My lifestyle/dress

Newspapers

Comedians

My religion

The books I read

School teachers

My sexual identity and outlook

My peer group

My sexual experiences

My ideas about morality

My friends

My parents

Openness to different ideas

The films/TV I have seen

Figure 6.1 *Some of the factors which are likely to influence the way we think about our own and others' sexuality*

alcohol were repealed and what had been considered immoral and corrupt became acceptable and even encouraged almost overnight.

- Most people would agree that it is an absolute and incontestable wrong to take the life of another (other than in direct self-defence) and if you murder someone you can rightly expect to be arrested and tried for a criminal act. But this view of *wrong* becomes adjusted during wartime, when killing other people who have been labelled 'the enemy' is regarded by society as a duty and not a crime.

Both these examples show how views of what is right and wrong can be changed to suit the needs of society: as such they cannot at the same time be 'absolute truths'. Many people see this argument as just as valid for ideas of right and wrong concerning a gay or lesbian sexual orientation.

There are examples of places around the world where being gay or lesbian is considered an acceptable and natural part of social life. For example, some parts of the USA such as Greenwich Village in New York and parts of

attitudes and beliefs *do* differ between cultures

the Florida Keys have thriving and long established gay and lesbian communities.

Labelling

being gay or lesbian is not just to do with having sex

We have used the terms gay man and lesbian freely in this and in other parts of the book to describe a form of sexual orientation where someone takes a person of the same sex to be their partner. Now while this term is probably quite acceptable to people who have adopted this type of lifestyle, it is not without its problems in that it is at the same time both too limiting and too all-inclusive.

It is too limiting because, by trying to define it, we are in danger of suggesting that being a gay man or a lesbian is only about a sexual relationship. This is not true. As with all types of relationships, gay and lesbian relationships are as much to do with love, friendship, sharing, trust and mutual interest as they are to do with sex. Equally, as with relationships between men and women, sex *is* an important but not the only important element in a gay or lesbian relationship.

labels cloud a person's other attributes

It is too all-inclusive because, by using the label gay man or lesbian, we run the risk of focusing only upon the person's sexual orientation and ignoring other important things about them, for example their abilities, contribution to society, politics or interests.

That's the problem with labels. They don't tell us enough but at the same time they categorize people, often in heavily negative terms, allowing us to fill in the gaps by using all sorts of stereotypes. Because of this we often find it difficult to see beyond the label and because of our existing prejudices, we don't really even want to try.

most people are not judged by their sexual orientation

If you are not a gay man or a lesbian, the chances are that your sexual orientation, because it is considered 'normal' by you and by others, is not a conscious part of the way you see yourself. You simply take it for granted. You are allowed to do this because your sexual orientation is not the factor by which others judge you. They will take you on your merits and abilities without ever questioning your choice of partner. Imagine what it would feel like if this were not the case, if other people judged you mostly in terms of your sexual orientation. While in your anger and frustration you might cry out 'But that's not the whole me, why not look at other equally significant aspects of who I am!', the chances are that others will choose not to hear you.

This problem of labelling is easily illustrated by considering people's reactions to those they know, who have 'come out' and declared themselves to be gay or lesbian. Not only do friends and relatives often say things like 'well I never knew she was like *that!*' to express their astonishment, they immediately start to look at and think about the person in new and different ways, which are often stereotypical and negative in nature. All too often, the person who has 'come out', does so at the risk of no longer being thought a good citizen, a good friend, a good worker or a good parent.

Steve and Terry

To highlight some of the things we have discussed so far, let's look at the example of Steve and Terry. Steve is a gay man and Terry is a heterosexual man. Terry thinks:

an example of how labelling works in practice

> 'Steve's not the type of bloke you could have a chat about football with down the pub, is he?'

Actually, Steve likes nothing better than to have a few beers with his mates and he is a keen supporter of Tottenham Hotspur football club. What Terry seems to believe is that because Steve is gay he must necessarily have a form of lifestyle and interests which are totally different from his own. Terry thinks:

> 'I couldn't just go up and have a chat with him because all my mates will think I've become queer!'

By thinking this, Terry has his own decisions and behaviour decided for him by ideas of what his friends might think about him, instead of making up his own mind and being his own person. Such everyday thinking keeps people who are different from us in some way at a distance and makes it doubly difficult for them to become equal members of the community, and derogatory terms such as 'queer' add to this. Terry thinks:

> 'I hope he doesn't come over and try to chat me up!'

This is another popular misconception (a myth that needs busting!) which arises out of vulnerability and ignorance. Gay men and lesbians don't want to get every man or woman they meet into bed. They will quickly pick up on signals which tell them whether another person is gay or lesbian and besides, they will only find certain people attractive, in exactly the same way that heterosexual people do. Remember also that many gay men and lesbians are already in stable, long-term relationships.

CLOTHING AND LIFESTYLE

Myth

'All gay men are effeminate and all lesbians are butch.'

Myth-buster

One of the ways in which prejudices against gay men and lesbians are kept alive is by perpetuating the myth that gay men are effeminate and lesbians are butch. By clinging to these images of gay lifestyle and gender, the majority group (controlled mainly by heterosexual men) retain views about normality and masculinity as if they were the same thing and of normality and femininity as if these too were inseparable.

We spoke in Chapter 1 about the way in which vulnerability plays a key role as a common root cause of prejudice and here is an excellent example. To overcome what they feel is a threat to their masculinity posed by gay men, heterosexual men emphasize ideas which link being gay with a lack of masculinity. Entwined with this stereotype is also a false logic which argues that, as gay men are more like women than men it's not surprising that they like other men.

At the same time, a view of gay men as less than masculine serves to keep other men in their place by acting as a form of social control. Images of manliness become wrapped up in images of macho masculinity and deviation from this 'ideal' is then criticized and degraded as a sure sign of gay tendencies. This has the effect of forcing heterosexual men to exaggerate their masculinity as a sign of their heterosexual virility and potency, whilst portraying gay men as less than men and more like women (Segal, 1990).

In her book *Slow Motion* (1990), Lynne Segal offers an interesting link between the way in which gay men are derided and labelled in negative terms as effeminate (in other words being like women) and the way in which men see women. She argues: 'Homophobia [the fear of being in close proximity to a homosexual person] in its contempt for the "feminine" in men, simultaneously expresses (a degree of male) contempt for women.' In a similar way, the image of the butch lesbian serves to reinforce the male-dominated majority view that really women cannot do without men and that even in lesbian relationships they find themselves creating a butch female as a pretend man.

'Hang on', you might argue, 'you can't say that "camp" gay men and butch lesbians are not an actual part of the gay and lesbian scene!' OK, we can't and won't say that. But what we will and must point out is that what these aspects of gay and lesbian culture mean to the people themselves is *not the same* as what the commonly held negative stereotypes would have us believe.

For instance, part of the meaning of the camp gay man image is a form of demonstration against the *falseness* of macho masculinity and a celebration of a form of sexual lifestyle that is free from the controlling and smothering influences of fixed gender stereotypes (fixed ideas about what men and women should be like). Still another part of its meaning may be as a parody or send-up of those very prejudices which emphasize the effeminacy of gay men. Seen from this viewpoint the camp gay male is a *reaction against* rather than a confirmation of what we believe to be the case. The ultra-macho biker/body-builder image, also found as part of the gay scene, suggests further parody of and reaction against the question of gay masculinity, but from the other end of the argument. These misunderstood aspects of gay and lesbian culture may have inadvertently strengthened the following myth.

Myth

'You can always tell when a person is gay or lesbian by the clothes they wear or by their mannerisms and lifestyle.'

Myth-buster

Such generalities, like other prejudices, have little basis in reality and are views based on labels about gay men and lesbians which, as we have seen, tell us next to nothing about individual people. Indeed, people from all walks of life, from all parts of the community, from all types of occupation and from all social and ethnic groups are gay.

GAY AND LESBIAN RELATIONSHIPS

Myth

'Gay men and lesbians do not have stable and long-lasting relationships in the way that heterosexual couples do.'

Myth-buster

This argument has been put forward as another attempt to show how this sexual lifestyle has grown out of an absence of morals and deviation from normal and acceptable behaviour. Gay men and to a lesser extent lesbians are depicted as promiscuous, driven not by love and friendship but by a search for purely sexual pleasure.

The reality actually differs little from patterns of heterosexual relationships. Both types of sexual lifestyle display a mixture of stable and long-lasting, settled relationships, as well as shorter-term 'flings'. Most married couples can tell of a series of boyfriends and girlfriends leading up to the point at which they came together and entered into a stable long-lasting relationship with each other.

It is also true that just as gay and lesbian relationships break down, so too do heterosexual relationships and marriages. And of course the search for sexual pleasure is as much a feature of heterosexual lifestyles as it is for homosexual ones. Images of how gay and lesbian relationships differ from heterosexual ones in terms of their lack of permanence and absence of love and friendship are very much part of the ongoing prejudice directed against members of the gay community, prejudice which seeks to isolate and distance them from the heterosexual majority.

LACK OF EQUALITY

equal
opportunities
are not a
reality for many
gay men and
lesbians

Being treated equally and fairly is all about having the same opportunities as everyone else and being dealt with as an individual on your own merits and abilities, enjoying the same respect and courtesy as the majority. It's also about freedom from prejudice, negative labelling and stereotyping. Unfortunately, as we have seen above, gay men and lesbians are still a very long way from being able to enjoy equal opportunities and fair treatment. Let's look at a few examples.

public displays
of affection, for
example, are
seen by some
as offensive

Gay men and lesbians are not able openly to display affection towards each other in public. If they indulge in the types of hand-holding and kissing that heterosexual couples do when out shopping or on the tube, in restaurants or at the cinema, the chances are that a complaint will be made against them, probably to the police. The result could be that their behaviour becomes interpreted as offensive, and they could be arrested! The result is that gay men and lesbians often hide their relationships behind closed doors and are made to feel guilt and shame.

Pause for thought

Take a few moments to imagine how you would feel if you were not allowed to openly display any love and affection towards your partner in public places and might face being arrested by the police if you did.

Many gay men and lesbians have found that if their sexual orientation becomes known to their employer, their career prospects become threatened. They may even find themselves subject to strategies and practices aimed at forcing them to leave. The fact that they were considered a good and respected worker before knowledge of their sexual orientation came to notice is quickly forgotten. Even where it is kept secret, informal expectations such as the expectation that employers should bring their partner to company social functions, for example, can prove uncomfortable, frustrating and embarrassing. 'Being a homosexual may not affect one's ability to do office work, but to be known as a homosexual in an office may make it impossible to continue working there' (Becker, 1963).

career
prospects may
be threatened

For gay men, the issue of the legal age of consent remains an example of institutionalized prejudice. In 1995 the age was lowered from 21 to 18 years but this is still, of course, out of line with the age of consent for heterosexual men (currently 16 years).

ages of consent
differ

Currently, a lot of controversy surrounds the issue of whether gay men and lesbians should be allowed custody of children and whether they should be allowed to become foster or adoptive parents. It is hardly surprising, given that, as we have seen, the majority group holds images of gay men and lesbians as sexual perverts and deviants, that they should at the same time question their suitability as parents. Again, such prejudices and discrimination arise out of vulnerability. The perceived threat on this occasion is that gay men and lesbians will somehow corrupt children's morals and lead them into a homosexual lifestyle. What evidence there is provides no support for such a view.

custody of children may be more difficult

The fact that a gay man or lesbian, while keeping their sexual orientation from view within a heterosexual marriage, is viewed as a good parent who loves their children, soon becomes forgotten once the parent chooses openly to declare their sexual orientation. The new label of them as a gay man or a lesbian often completely obscures these other aspects of who the person is, their abilities, their worth and their individuality.

Elsewhere in this book we have described legislation which aims to put the weight of the law behind combating prejudice and unfairness. The Sex Discrimination Act 1975 and the Race Relations Act 1976 are examples of such laws. But there is *no* such legislation to protect gay men and lesbians, and while many organizations include sexual orientation in their equal opportunity statements, such commitment lacks the force that the law could provide.

no legal protection from inequality

Pause for thought

We have raised a number of ways in which gay men and lesbians face a lack of equality in our society. Thinking about these, try and answer the following questions:

- Can you think of other ways, not already mentioned, in which gay men and lesbians might experience a lack of fair treatment and less than equal opportunities?
- What could be done in order to overcome such inequality and absence of fair treatment?
- Can you identify forms of more direct prejudice and discrimination that gay men and lesbians might face?

DIRECT PREJUDICE AND DISCRIMINATION

Although we have raised a number of ways in which gay men and lesbians can and do experience less than fair treatment and a direct lack of equal opportunity, there are forms of discrimination of a more immediate and threatening kind. Daily in this country gay men and lesbians are having to face open hostility and hatred which can range from simple avoidance to name-calling and abuse right through to threats of violence and actual attacks

anti-gay violence is not uncommon

and even murder. So-called 'queer-bashing' remains a real and ongoing threat to gay people, particularly in areas where gay clubs and bars are situated.

Gay men and lesbians argue that this direct and open hostility is not being given a high enough priority by the police who, it is claimed, because of their own prejudices, are not prepared to acknowledge the elements of discrimination that such threats and attacks contain or the very real consequences that such incidents have for gay men and lesbians in our community.

A FINAL WORD

Before leaving this section, we would like you to consider the thoughts of a woman who, when asked if she considered that being a lesbian was an exciting lifestyle, said:

> 'I think that not being able to move freely through society as a human being and a person with dignity isn't exciting. I think maybe robbing a bank is exciting, but not being an outcast because you have prefer- ences that the majority don't have, that's not exciting – it never was for me. I don't want to offend anybody, I just want to be a person. I just want to walk through life freely and not harm anybody. I don't want to be harmed, I just want to have fun. I don't want to think "Oh, there's something wrong with me, I'm not as good as this person, that I have to sit at the end of the table or have to go to the back of the bus", that sucks!'

KEY POINTS IN THIS CHAPTER

- The more strongly you disagree with another person's lifestyle, attitudes and values and the more negative you feel about them as a person, the more likely it is that you will hold extreme negative attitudes and preju- dices about them.
- Commonly held images of gay men and lesbians tend to be almost totally negative and derogatory.
- Being gay or lesbian is not an illness, nor is it a form of psychiatric condition for which people should be treated and from which they can recover.
- Attitudes that suggest gay men and lesbians are sexual deviants forget to explain that this form of sexual lifestyle only deviates from views of right and wrong (and of what is considered to be morally correct and acceptable behaviour) which are *constructed* by the majority group.
- These ideas of normal, acceptable, right and wrong are not fixed and self-apparent truths but are *flexible, relative and changing.*

- Our views about gay men and lesbians and, the images we hold seldom come from direct experience – instead they are given to us by our family, friends and teachers and from sources such as newspapers, magazines, TV, radio and film, etc.
- The labels typically applied to gay men and lesbians are very *unhelpful and limiting*. They tend to emphasize a few negative ideas but push other important parts of the person's identity and abilities from view.
- The camp gay man, the ultra-macho gay man and the butch lesbian are demonstrating *against* stereotypical images which claim they either lack masculinity (gay men) or cannot do without men (lesbians).
- Ideas that gay relationships are short-term and gay men and lesbians promiscuous have no basis in reality and serve only to keep prejudice alive.
- Gay men and lesbians suffer many forms of inequality including not being able to display affection in public, a higher age of consent (for men) and a closing off of employment opportunities. In addition they are less likely to be seen as suitable parents and guardians of the young.
- Gay men and lesbians continue to face open hostility and hatred which may amount to name-calling and abuse but could also include threats of violence, assault and even murder.

PERSONAL ACTION PLAN

Try answering the following questions:

How will the things I have learnt in this chapter change the way I think and act towards others who are different to me?

What has this chapter helped me to learn about myself with regard to:

- my beliefs;
- my attitudes;
- my values;
- my knowledge of others;
- my behaviour;
- my use of language;
- my responsibilities;
- the way I see the world?

How do I need to change in order to become:

- fairer;
- more sensitive;

- more understanding;
- less prejudicial;
- less discriminatory;
- better able to deal with people according to their needs?

If I were to change one thing about the way I act as a result of reading this chapter what would it be?

Chapter 7

Disability

It is estimated that there may be as many as 6 million people in the UK with some form of disability, a figure which represents almost 14 per cent of the population. It is not hard to see, therefore, that forms of prejudice and discrimination against those with disabilities can upset the lives of many people. Within this part of the book we shall look in some detail at how people who are disabled in some way can become marginalized and isolated by the attitudes of others and further disabled by the very environment in which they live and work.

By the time you have read this chapter we hope you will have a better understanding of the following issues:

- the types of insensitivity, prejudice and discrimination suffered by people who are disabled;
- common insensitivity towards people with a disability and how to avoid it;
- the disabling environment;
- issues concerning wheelchair users;
- issues concerning people who are blind or partially sighted; and
- issues concerning people who are deaf or who have hearing impairment.

A BRIEF WORD ABOUT TERMS AND LABELS

Throughout this book we have talked about the dangers of labelling people, a process by which we attach a name or label to a person because of a particular characteristic that they hold and then proceed to make all sorts of assumptions about them based on that label. Not only do labels give rise to such fixed thinking, they also make us forget many other important things about the person or group of people we are talking about. The word 'disabled' is a label and it can conjure up all sorts of fixed ways of thinking about those we call disabled. In particular the term carries with it ideas of helplessness and dependence – we shall explore these issues later in the chapter.

Because the term 'disabled' is commonly used both by able-bodied and less able people, we have used it in this book to avoid a clumsy style of writing that may lack meaning for the reader. What we would ask you to

labels breed fixed thinking

keep in mind is that whether a person is a wheelchair user, or is deaf or blind, these disabilities only make the person less able to do certain things – it doesn't and shouldn't disqualify them from being a full and valued member of the community.

TYPES OF INSENSITIVITY, PREJUDICE AND DISCRIMINATION

disability may be more about others' attitudes and the environment

When we think about people with disabilities it's easy to assume that what we identify as their disability, the fact that they are in a wheelchair for example, is *the* thing that will cause them problems in their daily life, but this may be only partly true. While their disability may mean that they have had to adapt the way they think about and do things day to day, it is more likely that those with a disability become most disabled by the attitudes that others hold about them and by the environment in which they live. We will talk in more detail about the disabling environment later in this chapter, so let's turn now to the question of attitudes and insensitivity.

Pause for thought

Think for a moment about your own attitudes towards disabled people and the reactions of others that you may have seen or heard.

- How do you, or other people, typically react when they pass by a person who is disabled in some way?
- How do you, or other people, typically react when introduced to a disabled person?
- Can you identify typical forms of insensitivity that people may display towards a person who is disabled?

---

again the problem is about what is considered 'normal' by society

It's likely that if you're not disabled yourself you carry around ideas of what it is to be 'normal' and these ideas will include assumptions that to be normal is to be able-bodied. Even if you feel that this isn't true for you it's certainly how most people think and so it's not surprising that when people see someone who is disabled they tend to react. These reactions might easily include any or all of the following:

- They stand and stare.
- They stop talking.
- They may point the person out to a friend.
- They may talk behind their hand to a friend while indicating the person who is disabled with a nod or a stare.

- People will move away.
- Parents may even gather their children around them.

You may even be able to think of other reactions you have seen yourself. The point is that, sadly, disability is a stigma, a mark which sets the person apart from 'the rest of us' (Goffman, 1990). Such reactions are hurtful and enforce a feeling of isolation and separateness – it's as if the able-bodied are saying 'you shouldn't come here and mix with us, you should keep yourself to yourself, that way you don't become a burden for the rest of us to deal with'. This feeling is captured in the following experience – a man who's blind has gone to the barber for a haircut:

> The [barber's] shop was hushed and solemn as I was ushered in and I was virtually lifted by the uniformed attendant into the chair. I tried a joke, the usual thing about getting a haircut once every three months even if I didn't need it. It was a mistake. The silence told me that I wasn't a man who should make jokes, not even good ones (quoted in Chevigny, 1962: 68).

an example of a blind man in a barber's shop

In Chapters 1 and 2 we stressed how the appropriate use of empathy was a core and transferable skill in extending equal opportunities and fair treatment to everybody, and it is certainly of value here. By imagining how you would feel as a disabled person in these circumstances you will quickly realize what it might feel like to be in just such a situation with people staring, pointing or distancing themselves from you.

Other reactions which disabled people often face represent the other side of the coin to those we have already mentioned above and include oversensitivity, pity and patronizing comments and attitudes. Rather than give examples of this form of prejudice we feel it is better to offer you, the reader, guidance on how to avoid such pitfalls. We do this below in the section about avoiding common forms of insensitivity towards disabled people.

other equality unwelcome reactions include pity

Discrimination in employment and education

Prejudice towards the disabled quickly becomes discrimination in other areas such as access to employment, education and other public amenities.

Employment

Being less than fully able can often prove a bar to many forms of employment where employers either cannot or, more often, will not take on a disabled person for particular types of work. Common arguments offered by employers include:

- A disabled person would not be capable of undertaking the work advertised.

Apart from work with specific physical requirements that would directly rule out certain disabled people, advances in technology will increasingly enable those with disabilities to work comfortably alongside their able-bodied colleagues doing the same jobs.

- It would prove too expensive to adapt working conditions to allow them necessary access or facilities to do the job.

The whole issue of having to make adjustments to the places that disabled people work and the way that their work is arranged has recently become a legal responsibility placed on employers by the Disability Discrimination Act. Also, there is a growing awareness amongst architects that building designs which provide good access for the disabled also improve overall ease of use for everyone.

arguments against employing disabled people usually have no basis in fact

As we have already said, the stigma which so often accompanies disability prevents disabled people from securing other forms of work which require direct contact with the public. Employers, fearing that disabled employees will turn customers away, will not employ them in such positions irrespective of their abilities to do the job. How many wheelchair users have you come across who are till operators in supermarkets, or teachers or librarians or solicitors? Why is this? It rarely needs to be because the person is a wheelchair user!

Education

People with disabilities may also face discrimination in the area of education. Often, the specific needs of blind or deaf people, for example, are only met through the provision of 'special' schools and, while such schools may do an excellent job, it does mean that rather than integrating with 'mainstream' students, those with disabilities are kept apart, and this tends to reinforce attitudes of separateness.

separateness is still reinforced in education

Such problems become even more acute in further or higher education (colleges and universities) where, although some improvements have been made for wheelchair access, few offer facilities for deaf and blind students at an effective level. This lack of facilities and support discourages people with disabilities from pursuing their education and reinforces the message that society sees their specific needs as a burden that is either too costly or involves too much effort to meet. It is hoped that provisions within the Disability Discrimination Act that require colleges and universities to examine and improve their existing arrangements and facilities for disabled students will promote much-needed improvements in this area.

Pause for thought

If you are a student either at school or at college or university see if you can find out the following:

- What provisions does your place of education have for wheelchair users, or people who are blind or deaf?
- What percentage of students at your place of education are disabled?
- Does your school, college or university have an equal opportunities policy? If it does, is disability mentioned?

HOW TO AVOID COMMON INSENSITIVITY

We have already spoken of the typical reactions of people who see a disabled person – remind yourself of these points before we move on. We hope that, having read this book, *your* reactions will be modified as necessary and based on empathy (thinking how you might feel in the person's position) and sensitivity (realizing how such reactions must make the person feel). *be aware of insensitive attitudes and behaviour*

In addition to these reactions are many other forms of insensitivity which become apparent when people meet or are introduced to a person who has a disability, and these can best be grouped under three headings.

Insensitive language

There are plenty of expressions which are clearly inappropriate, insulting and hurtful such as 'blind as a bat', 'deaf as a post', 'cripple', 'mutt'n'jeff', 'spasmo' as well as common terms which, while not meant to be hurtful, are still insensitive, these include 'deaf and dumb', 'handicapped' and 'invalid'. We will be returning to some of these expressions later in this chapter to consider why they might be inappropriate and inaccurate. *. . . language*

Being over-sensitive

We all value our freedom and independence and would probably feel quite put out if other people thought they knew what was best for us, or fussed unduly, offering to do things which we felt more than capable of doing for ourselves. This is as true, if not more so, for people who are living with a disability. They will have worked hard to adjust the way they think about and do things to take account of their disability and may not take too kindly to being viewed as helpless, dependent or pathetic. *. . . being patronizing*

By the same token there will be times when all of us struggle from time to time and a kindly offer of assistance from someone else is not only appropriate but welcome. This is true for everyone, whether able-bodied or disabled in some way. The thing to remember, if you feel that someone *. . . we all have the right to refuse help* might like your help, is to offer assistance politely and not to be offended if it is refused. Chances are that the disabled person is far more able than you might first assume them to be.

Returning to the question of language for a moment, there are expressions which crop up in everyday language which are quite acceptable to disabled people and will not cause offence. For instance blind people will say 'be seeing you' to others in conversation and will not be upset if you use this in conversation. Other similar phrases include 'did you hear about . . .' or 'I must be running along'.

Pity

. . . pity

Another way in which people can be insensitive is by saying things which amount to pity towards the person who is disabled. Try to avoid saying things like: 'you poor thing', 'it must be awful for you', 'how do you cope?', or 'who looks after you?' Such phrases are not helpful and do *not* convey the warmth and support that they suggest. Instead they can reinforce the difference between the able-bodied person and the subject of their unwanted pity . . . in effect it's like saying 'how awful that you're not like me'.

THE DISABLING ENVIRONMENT

Everywhere you look and in all aspects of social and working life, arrangements and designs serve the able-bodied majority. Think about the following examples:

- aisles in shops;
- corridors in offices;
- width of doors;
- the height of public phone-boxes and other public amenities;
- the absence of text telephones for the deaf;
- the absence of ramps;
- the scarcity of lifts;
- the huge number of visual signs for directing and warning;
- the design of buses and trains;
- obstacles on walkways and pavements such as badly parked cars, broken or uneven paving and roadworks; and
- the fact that wheelchair users must book their journey in advance if they want to travel by underground (they are considered a fire risk!).

it is the
environment that
disables many
people

This is just a small list and you will undoubtedly be able to think about many more examples of how the built environment is a huge disabling factor in the lives of disabled people. In fact we would go as far as to say that it is the way that the able-bodied majority arranges the built environment which disables people who themselves have learnt to adapt themselves to their disability.

For example, deaf people have a highly developed language using signs rather than words and this language is as rich and varied and as powerful as spoken English or any other language. What prevents them from being able to communicate freely with hearing people is the fact that few hearing people know how to sign. If more people learned sign language the easier it would be for all of us to communicate with each other.

There are some indications that things in the built environment are improving. In some places, such as new shopping centres, access for wheelchair users has been greatly improved with the provision of ramps, lifts and wider walkways and aisles. Interestingly, parents with children in pushchairs are also enjoying these improvements. Public telephones are also beginning to include one handset at a lower level, and we have even seen the odd public text telephone.

Some bus companies are beginning to use new types of bus which lower themselves at bus stops and have a special ramp entrance in the middle for wheelchair users.

Finally, the increased use of e-mail, the Internet and the World Wide Web together with both online (Internet) shopping and banking and interactive TV has started to offer new opportunities for those who have hearing or mobility problems. Speech programs which allow your computer to talk to you, as well as other accessibility options for the computer, similarly promise the freedom of the Internet and the World Wide Web to an even larger number of disabled persons.

ISSUES CONCERNING WHEELCHAIR USERS

Myth

'Because a person is in a wheelchair it must mean they aren't as "with it" and as intelligent as an able-bodied person.'

Myth-buster

A person may be in a wheelchair for many different reasons and if their need for a wheelchair arises from a physical disability it is clearly ridiculous to suggest that their wheelchair use must mean they are not as mentally able and as clever as any able-bodied person. You only have to look at Stephen Hawking, the famous astrophysicist, to realize how wrong such assumptions can be.

What seems to happen is that because a person uses a wheelchair they are valued less as an individual and ignored, patronized, pitied or avoided by others who wrongly presume that because they themselves are able-bodied, this somehow makes them superior and of more value as a person than a person in a wheelchair. As a result the wheelchair user has to work harder just to be accepted as a 'normal' person and to prove themselves to be of equal value.

The classic example of this is where a wheelchair user and an able-bodied friend go to the counter of a cafe for a cup of tea and, as the able-bodied person is in the process of ordering the refreshments, the person serving them nods towards the wheelchair user and asks 'does he take sugar?' Even in this short exchange we can see a wealth of prejudice and stereotyping revealed:

- The person serving them assumes the person in the wheelchair cannot answer for themselves.
- The wheelchair user's identity is totally wrapped up in their disability and the person serving cannot see beyond this.
- The person serving presumes the person in the wheelchair is dependent on their able-bodied companion.
- There is an assumption that an intelligent reply may only be forthcoming from the able-bodied person.
- The person serving is more comfortable speaking to another 'normal' person.

Being more aware of the needs of people who are wheelchair users

From the example above we hope you will see that a person does not lose their individuality, their independence and their value as a person because they happen to use a wheelchair. As such, the first thing you should keep in mind is that here is a person just like you who just happens to need a wheelchair to get around. This person has exactly the same right to be treated fairly and with respect and courtesy as everyone else, and you shouldn't allow the wheelchair to become a barrier to this (see Figure 7.1).

In terms of the wheelchair itself and the person's use of it, you should also consider the following points:

- Don't lean on the wheelchair, either when talking to the person using it or when talking to someone else.
- Don't put things like jackets or coats on the wheelchair – the wheelchair is personal to the user and is not a coat-rack.
- When speaking with someone in a wheelchair it is more polite if you can crouch down or, better still, sit down so that you can be at their eye level when talking with them.

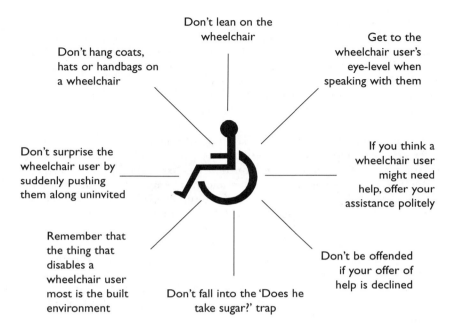

Figure 7.1 *Some useful things to remember when talking with or offering assistance to a wheelchair user*

- Don't surprise the wheelchair user by suddenly grabbing the wheelchair and pushing them along. This would be a bit like having someone grab you by the elbow and push you along without you expecting it.
- If you think a wheelchair user would appreciate help, offer it politely and seek directions from them about what help is needed. Don't get upset if your offer of help is not accepted.
- Be aware of inappropriate language. Words such as 'cripple' or 'spas' are offensive. The word 'invalid' suggests that person is not a valid individual. The word 'handicapped' derives from the expression 'cap-in-hand' and suggests the wheelchair user is dependent on others and as such lacks valuable independence and freedom.

ISSUES CONCERNING PEOPLE WHO ARE BLIND OR PARTIALLY SIGHTED

You will notice from the title of this section that it is quite inaccurate to assume that all people who are disabled because they have visual impairment are necessarily blind. Some may, in fact, be partially sighted.

advice about
offering help to
blind or partially
sighted people

It is estimated that in the UK there are over 275,000 people who are registered blind or partially sighted and it's worth stressing that most of these people make use of shops, public transport and other public facilities in the same way that their sighted neighbours do. Remember too that not all blind or partially sighted people have access to a guide dog (not all necessarily want to) and that whether they have or not, there will be times when, like any of us, a person who is visually disabled needs help because they feel lost.

Much of this section will be taken up with advice concerning how to offer effective help *when it's needed* and how to extend empathy by giving useful commentary and information that will assist the blind or partially sighted person to regain their bearings and avoid embarrassment. We would like to acknowledge the agency 'Action for Blind People' (their details appear in Chapter 10) for information which assisted us in the compilation of much of this section.

> Crowded streets, poor paving, drop kerbs, badly parked cars ... there are many hazards to be negotiated. It is important therefore, that assistance is offered where needed and that it is a help not a hindrance (*Guiding Blind and Partially Sighted People,* Action for Blind People information pamphlet).

People can often feel embarrassed or reluctant to offer help fearing they may be doing or may say the wrong thing. However, if you see a person who is blind or partially sighted who looks as if they need help, politely introduce yourself and offer your assistance. Don't grab their arm and don't raise your voice (you may laugh, but this is a common reaction; the fact that a person is visually disabled doesn't mean that they have problems hearing as well).

Be guided by what the person wants, and if they don't need your help don't be offended. At the same time don't assume you know where the person wants to go by the direction they are facing – ask.

If the person is happy to accept your offer of assistance consider the following points:

- Ask the person if they would like to take your arm. If they do they will probably grip it lightly just above the elbow. This will be your 'guiding arm' and you should try to keep it straight by your side. Do *not* take the person's arm and propel them along.
- Once you have agreed where you are going, start off slowly and keep at a modest pace which feels comfortable and safe. Watch out for things which may get in the person's path as you guide them – a gentle commentary would help, informing the person of any obstacles before you both reach them.

- If you approach steps tell the person this and say whether they go up or down. Tell them if there is a banister rail and walk so that the person can make use of it if they so wish. Tell them when you reach the bottom, take a small step forward and then pause to allow the person to descend the last step.
- If you have to cross a road explain how the traffic is moving and leave a sufficient gap to allow both of you to cross at a modest pace.
- If in a busy street it is necessary for you both to walk in single file, indicate this by moving the hand of your guiding arm to the small of your back. Once the need for this has passed you can move your guiding arm back to your side. Once again, talk to the other person, explaining what you are doing and why.
- If you need to help a blind or partially sighted person to sit down, place their hand gently on the back of the chair, telling what you are doing and why, *before* you do it.

Some other general points to bear in mind include introducing yourself when you meet a person who is blind or partially sighted and introducing others with you, saying where they are standing in relation to you, for example 'and this is Steve Baxter, who is on my right'.

ISSUES CONCERNING PEOPLE WHO ARE PROFOUNDLY OR PARTIALLY DEAF

Myth

'If a person can't hear it's typical that they can't speak as well, after all that's the condition isn't it?. . . Deaf and dumb.'

Myth-buster

We live in a world of verbal communication where the ability to talk with others and listen to their replies is considered a basic essential of social life. If you were to reflect on what is a typical day for you, the chances are that you will spend a fair proportion of it engaged in chatting with family, friends, work colleagues and other people you may come into contact with. Consider then what impact being deaf might have on your everyday life – you would find it extremely difficult if not impossible to communicate effectively with other people.

For those people who have been deaf from birth, the problem of communication in a hearing world extends to speech as well, because even though such people have the ability to speak (they are not dumb as is commonly suggested in the term deaf and dumb) having never heard speech they have no understanding of what words sounds like and how to form them. Following prolonged and difficult training however, many people who have been deaf from birth (or from an early age) do learn to speak.

Nonetheless, because their speech may not be as clear and well structured as that of a hearing person, it is all too easy for people to make the assumption that deaf people lack intelligence. Now that you, the reader, realize the difficulty of learning a language you have never heard, you will be in a position to put such prejudiced thinking behind you.

Sign language and finger spelling

The deaf community, which can be thought of as including people who are both profoundly deaf (fully deaf) and those who have partial hearing loss, have developed their own visual language which is as rich, descriptive and powerful as any spoken language. You have probably seen sign language used along with spoken language on news and current affairs programmes on television. Like any full-blown language, sign language has developed local dialects and people who are deaf and who live and work in London may, for example, have the same difficulty understanding certain signs used by a deaf person who lives in the North of England as a hearing person might with some spoken northern dialects.

sign language

Because the term 'deaf person' has such a broad application, it is probably more accurate to understand the term as referring not to a particular physical condition, but instead as signalling membership of an identifiable linguistic and cultural group. Take a look at the poem below which was written by a person who is deaf.

YOU HAVE TO BE DEAF TO UNDERSTAND
(extracts from a poem by Willard J. Madsen)

What is it like to 'hear' a hand?
You have to be deaf to understand

What is it like to be shouted at
When someone thinks that will help you to hear
Or misunderstands the words of a friend
Who is trying to make a joke clear
And you don't get the point because he's failed
You have to be deaf to understand

What is it like to be laughed in the face
When you try to repeat what is said
Just to make sure that you've understood

And you find that the words were misread
And you want to cry out 'Please help me my friend!'
You have to be deaf to understand

What is it like to be deaf and alone
In the company of those who can hear
And you can only guess as you go along
For no one's there with a helping hand
As you try to keep up with the words of a song
You have to be deaf to understand

What is it like to comprehend
Some nimble fingers that paint the scene
And make you smile and feel serene
With the 'Spoken word' of the moving hand
That makes you part of the world at large
You have to be deaf to understand

What is it like to 'hear' a hand
Yes, you have to be deaf to understand!

The main form of sign language used by deaf people in this country is British Sign Language or BSL, and most colleges and evening classes offer courses where you can go and learn how to sign. It is both an interesting and rewarding thing to do. It is important to realize that British Sign Language is *not* a system where spoken words have become translated into individual signs; instead, BSL has developed (and will continue to develop) as a complete visual language. As such there are signs for which there is no corresponding spoken alternative, just as there are spoken words for which there is no signed alternative.

British Sign Language

Alternatively you could begin by learning the slower but more straight-forward system of finger spelling. We have included a diagram (Figure 7.2) with permission from the British Deaf Association which shows you the correct finger positions and their relative meanings. All you do, having learned the finger spellings, is to join them together to make the words you want. You will see that spelling words a letter at a time can be a far more time-consuming business than using a single sign for a given word or phrase, however.

Lip-reading

Another skill that a person who is deaf might develop is lip-reading, the ability to comprehend what a hearing person is saying by interpreting their lip movements and patterns. Try it yourself. Even when people are speaking slowly and you know basically what they are taking about, working out what they are saying from watching their lip movements is *very* difficult and

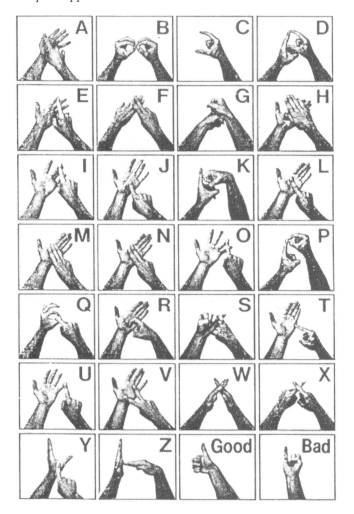

Figure 7.2   *British two-handed fingerspelling*

demands great concentration. It's likely that you will pick up little of what they actually say, although you might catch the broad drift of the conversation. Of course, if you don't know the context you will probably fail to capture anything they are saying and you will be left outside the conversation.

When a person who is deaf or partially deaf tries to lip-read what you are saying there are things that you can do that will help them (Figure 7.3) get the most from what you are trying to say:

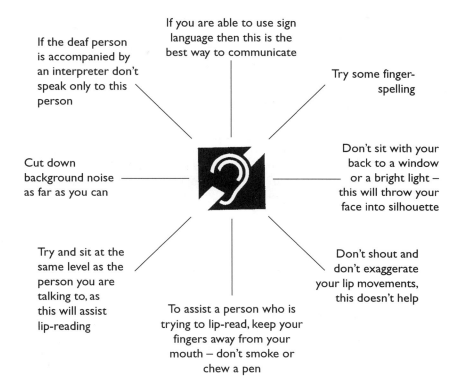

Figure 7.3   *Some useful things to remember when talking with a person who is profoundly or partially deaf*

- Don't sit near a window, as the light coming in may throw your face into silhouette and make lip-reading difficult.
- Don't exaggerate your lip movements, as this may lay false emphasis on what you are trying to say.
- Keep your hands and fingers away from your face and don't chew on a pen or pencil or smoke a cigarette as you are talking.
- Sit at the same level and facing the person who is trying to lip-read from you.
- If appropriate don't feel afraid to show feeling in your facial and upper body gestures, as people trying to lip-read will pick up not only on your lip movements but also on supporting body language.
- Try to cut down background noise, as the person who is lip-reading may have some hearing and may use this to support information gained from watching your lip movements and gestures.
- If you or the other person turns away, stop talking, as they will miss parts of your conversation.

- Keep what you are trying to say reasonably straightforward – long or complex words may not be understood.
- If the deaf person is accompanied by a hearing friend try to avoid talking exclusively to that person just because it's easier for you.

KEY POINTS IN THIS CHAPTER

- People who are disabled often face hurtful and offensive reactions from people who have little sensitivity or empathy. Empathy and greater understanding can help you avoid adding to such prejudice.
- People who are disabled are sometimes made to feel they are intruding into the world of the able-bodied majority. This isolates them from the communities in which they live.
- It is the built environment (steps, narrow corridors, voice public phones, visual signs, etc.) that has the effect of disabling people who have restricted mobility or have a visual or hearing impairment.
- In the area of employment, people who are disabled face arguments that they are incapable of doing proper jobs, that their contact with the customer would lose sales or that it would cost too much money to alter working arrangements to meet their needs.
- In the area of education there is little effective provision for students who are deaf or blind and there are only limited arrangements to improve access for students who are wheelchair users.
- Too often a person's disability is all that able-bodied people focus on – they ignore the real person who is at the same time disabled.
- Many people wrongly assume that because someone is disabled they must also be unintelligent.
- There are many ways in which you can assist a person who is deaf, blind or a wheelchair user but first you should ask the person if they need and want your help – they may not.

PERSONAL ACTION PLAN

Try answering the following questions:

How will the things I have learnt in this chapter change the way I think and act towards others who are different to me?

What has this chapter helped me to learn about myself with regard to:

- my beliefs;
- my attitudes;

- my values;
- my knowledge of others;
- my behaviour;
- my use of language;
- my responsibilities;
- the way I see the world?

How do I need to change in order to become:

- fairer;
- more sensitive;
- more understanding;
- less prejudicial;
- less discriminatory;
- better able to deal with people according to their needs?

If I were to change one thing about the way I act as a result of reading this chapter what would it be?

Chapter 8
Institutional Discrimination

One of the key debates in equal opportunities in 1999 was that generated by the public inquiry into the murder of a young black student named Stephen Lawrence and the publication of *The Macpherson Report* in February of the same year, which disclosed its findings. The police were severely criticized for the way that they had handled the investigation into Stephen's death. A central finding of the inquiry was that the police had been 'institutionally racist'.

The conclusions of the Stephen Lawrence inquiry concerning institutional discrimination have consequences for all of our large institutions such as education, health, social services and housing as well as for the police themselves.

Because of the fundamental importance of institutional discrimination and its impact on our society, we have devoted a separate chapter to it in order that the issues it raises can be examined in detail.

By the time you have finished reading through this chapter we hope you will:

- have gained a background knowledge of *The Macpherson Report* (1999) and some of the key issues it raised;
- be able to define the terms 'institution', 'institutional racism', 'sexism' and 'discrimination';
- be able to explain why the concepts are important for organizations and individuals committed to fairness and equality of opportunity;
- have thought about the implications for you and your own institution or organization.

THE STEPHEN LAWRENCE INQUIRY

Stephen Lawrence was a young black man who was murdered in a racist attack in south London on 22 April 1993. No one has ever been convicted of his murder, but pressure from his parents eventually led to a public inquiry, chaired by Sir William Macpherson.

A whole range of criticisms of the police investigation into the teenager's death were made during that inquiry but it was the identification of the part that institutional racism had to play that attracted most attention.

The report was published in a blaze of publicity and made 70 recommendations ranging from increased openness, accountability and the restoration of confidence in the police, to the prevention of racism through the role of education.

The Macpherson Report (chapter 46, paragraphs 25–28) concluded that there had been a 'catalogue of errors' (p. 321) that could only be accounted for in terms of something more than just incompetence on the part of the individuals involved. Institutional rather than individual racism was given as a key reason for the failure of the investigation. The police service was not alone in this, and a broader view was taken. As Macpherson observes:

The Macpherson Report made 70 recommendations

> We do not accept that a finding of institutional racism within the police service means that all officers are racist. We all agree that institutional racism affects the Metropolitan Police Service, and Police Services elsewhere. Furthermore, our conclusions about Police Services should not lead to complacency in other institutions and organisations. Collective failure is apparent in many of them, including the Criminal Justice System. It is incumbent on every institution to examine their policies and the outcome of their policies and practices to guard against disadvantaging any section of our communities.
>
> (Macpherson, 1999: 321)

Pause for thought

Re-read the above passage quoted directly from Macpherson and consider how it might relate to your own institution.

These were some of the problems the report identified as suggesting that institutional discrimination had taken place:

- insensitive and racially stereotypical behaviour at the scene of the murder leading to false assumptions being made;
- lack of family liaison and a failure to look after people according to their needs;
- failure through racial stereotyping to treat people properly as victims;
- refusal to accept that the crime being investigated was a racial murder;
- officers engaged in the investigation allowing their negative attitudes to influence the work they were doing;
- the use of inappropriate and offensive language.

evidence of institutional racism

You will notice that many of the problems identified by the report are themes we have covered throughout this book. These include the way stereotyping leads to assumptions about people who are different to us; inappropriate use of language that leads to offence and suggests racial prejudices and also the way that racist attitudes affected behaviour.

unwitting racism is evident in many institutions

The report pointed out that none of these things, in its view, resulted from the overt application of discrimination and disadvantage. The racism shown was unwitting (in the chapter on racism we raised the issue of unintentional racism). Although these instances of unwitting racism relate directly to a specific police investigation, it is not hard to draw parallels with other organizations and institutions.

Myth

'Institutional racism is a problem that only manifests itself in policing.'

Myth-buster

The police service never seems too far from the headlines when its relations with minority groups are concerned. Given the media coverage this generates, you could be forgiven for thinking that policing was the only institution guilty of institutional racism. This is not so. Macpherson (1999) notes that 'collective failure' in relation to institutional racism is apparent in many other organizations. Later in this chapter you will encounter examples from housing, education, social service provision and provisions and facilities for disabled people.

We will return to this later in the chapter when we consider the impact all this may have on equal opportunities generally.

INSTITUTIONAL RACISM, SEXISM AND DISCRIMINATION – THE THEORY

institutional racism is not a new concept

A surprising feature of the debate about institutional racism was that many people seemed to speak as if the concept was new and that it had somehow been invented as a political weapon with which to undermine organizations such as the police. In fact, the notion of institutional racism has been around for many years. The Metropolitan Police were themselves teaching the concept as part of their Human Awareness Programme in the early to mid-1980s. This section is about definitions and, as we will see in a moment, words do matter because it was the meanings that people were assigning to the words that caused a great deal of difficulty in finding common ground.

The meaning of 'institution'

As it transpired (see below) *The Macpherson Report* did not actually use the word 'institution' in its final definition. But many people, including the media still talk about 'institutional racism' or 'institutional discrimination', so it is important to know the range of meanings that the word has.

Generally speaking, the word 'institution' refers to a set of social practices that are regularly and continuously repeated so that they become formalized as the accepted way of doing something. They are the arrangements that a society develops to manage the daily lives of its members. These arrangements will include arrangements for policing, for dealing with people's health, for education and many others including housing, social services, justice and so on.

institutions are sets of social practices that become formalized

A single hospital would not be an institution, whereas the total system for delivering health care in this country and the way that this system is arranged and operates day-by-day certainly would be. It is the way in which such a service is arranged that can give rise to disadvantage and discrimination, despite the best efforts of the individuals within it.

These arrangements are complex, with systems of specialist personnel and support staff, technical words and phrases, systems of communications and set ways of seeing and solving problems, all of which have evolved over a long period of time. For example, policing in its current form is over 170 years old. These set ways of seeing and solving problems haven't always kept pace with changes in our diverse culture and may not always meet the needs of some members of our community; it is here that disadvantage and discrimination at an institutional level can occur.

ways of seeing the world and approaches to solving problems may not have changed for generations

In the case of Stephen Lawrence, the existing ways of solving his murder gave no account of the racist nature of this crime, and the ways in which officers had been taught to view, to investigate and to solve murders failed to take proper account of this crucial dimension.

Pause for thought

To a greater or lesser extent you will be involved with all the types of institution noted above at some time or other.

- First of all, think of specific institutions in one or more groups that you may be involved with. You could start with locating your job or main role in one of the groups. Example: 'I am a nurse – my institution is health.'
- Now try to think of some examples of the practices in that institution which you can identify as being regular and continuous. Example: 'We provide primary healthcare services to people – we do this by

running the clinic, admitting people to hospital for operations and after-care.'

• Hold these in your thoughts or make a note of them because later in the chapter you will be challenged to examine them for evidence of institutional discrimination.

accepted
practices and
norms may
create
disadvantage

So when we think about institutional discrimination, we are really focusing on the ways in which sets of accepted practices (typical ways of doing things within an institution) and norms (typical ways of thinking and behaving within an institution) create instances of disadvantage by discriminating against people or groups of people.

Of course, all of these institutions are composed of individuals but it is not, in fact, the individuals who are the focus here, but the norms and practices of the institution. This is a very important point which, if not understood, can lead to the myth below.

Myth

'If an organization is labelled institutionally discriminatory, then everyone in the organization must be intentionally discriminating.'

Myth-buster

One of the main obstacles to a rapid acceptance by the police of the label 'institutionally racist' was the inference that it necessarily meant that every individual in the police was racist. However, by thinking about the nature of institutions, we have seen that this is not the case.

Senior police officers were faced with a dilemma. If they admitted institutional racism they risked losing the confidence of individual officers who considered that they were doing their best to promote equal opportunities in the police, but misunderstood what institutional discrimination meant. If they refused to accept the label they would seem to have failed to heed the lessons coming out of the Stephen Lawrence inquiry.

In the event, Macpherson (the judge who chaired the inquiry) offered a definition of institutional discrimination which Sir Paul Condon (then the Commissioner of the Metropolitan Police Service) was able to accept and endorse publicly, as did a number of other Chief Constables.

Institutional racism

The Stephen Lawrence inquiry gave rise to an intense debate about the notion of institutional racism. A key reason for the fierceness of the debate arose from the fact that the police, as an institution that enforces the law, hold a lot of power. We have already seen earlier in this book that, where individuals who can exert power over others have prejudices that affect their actions, discrimination can result. This is just as true for institutions. Where a powerful institution maintains prejudicial arrangements, discrimination can and does occur.

powerful institutions are especially vulnerable

Pause for thought

We have spoken a lot about the police as an institution, but other institutions also have power over aspects of people's lives. Choose two institutions from the following list and consider what power they may have over you at some time in your life:

- education;
- health;
- politics;
- housing;
- social services.

During the chapter on racism we suggested that racism arises when a person or group of people are discriminated against on the basis of their ethnicity. When we talk about institutionalized racism, we mean that a person or group of people become discriminated against on the basis of their ethnicity as a result of the arrangements and accepted practices within an institution.

An example of a discriminatory practice within an institution would be if a local authority housing department were to require all ethnic minority families to produce their passports when applying for a council property to prove they were British citizens, but did not make that same requirement for white families.

The report that resulted from the public inquiry into the murder of Stephen Lawrence has created a new and detailed definition of what institutional discrimination is. By doing so, they hope to encourage all large institutions to examine their existing arrangements to ensure that they meet the needs of all members of the community and promote fairness and equality.

The report defines institutional discrimination as arising from:

definition of
institutional
racism

The collective failure of an organisation to provide an appropriate and professional service to people because of their colour, culture or ethnic origin. It can be seen or detected in processes, attitudes and behaviour which amount to discrimination through unwitting prejudice, ignorance, thoughtlessness and racist stereotyping which disadvantage minority ethnic people.

(Macpherson, 1999, para. 6.34, p. 28)

It is worth looking at some of the key words of the definition in a little more detail:

analysis of the
definition

- The failure is '*collective*' rather than individually focused.
- An '*appropriate service*' seems to suggest the need to meet people's individual needs.
- This failure on account of '*colour, culture [and] ethnic origin*' are all factors which make racism apparent. It is clear that the same could equally apply to women, members of the gay and lesbian community, people with disabilities and other groups who regularly experience prejudice and discrimination.
- '*Seen or detected*' seems to include the subtle as well as the obvious application of discrimination.
- '*Processes, attitudes and behaviour*' is interesting because the first relates to how the organization is, but the latter refer to the way individuals are. These amount to . . .
- '*Discrimination through unwitting prejudice, ignorance, thoughtlessness and racist stereotyping*'. It is not immediately clear from the definition whether it is just the prejudice that is unwitting and that the thoughtlessness, or racist stereotyping are more purposeful. However, the overall context of Macpherson's report suggests that it is meant that all the acts mentioned are taken as unwitting.

Pause for thought

If a person does something unwittingly – how much responsibility can they be expected to bear for their actions?

INSTITUTIONAL DISCRIMINATION – THE APPLICATION

Implications for policy and procedures

The key criticisms of the police investigation into Stephen's death included:

- insensitive and racially stereotypical behaviour;
- failure to keep in touch with Stephen's family and to seek their views;
- failure to look after people according to their needs;
- failure through racial or sexist stereotyping to treat people properly as victims;
- refusal to accept that the problem was racially motivated;
- people allowing their negative attitudes to influence the work they were doing;
- the use of inappropriate and offensive language.

key criticisms of the police investigation

Now look at these criticisms in the light of some of the activities that all institutions undertake. Think about how such racism might arise if these activities contained forms of discriminatory practice:

- recruitment of personnel;
- selection of personnel;
- retention of personnel;
- promotion opportunities;
- development opportunities;
- delivery of services or goods;
- the processes of your organization;
- training in your organization;
- morale in your organization.

Looking at your own organization or institution

In most, if not all of these areas of activity, your organization or institution will have policies and procedures. In order to avoid institutional discrimination it is important that all of these policies and procedures are examined closely for one of four things:

1. Do any of the policies and procedures directly discriminate against a particular group? An example would be selection criteria that could not be justified as a genuine occupational qualification and which operates directly to exclude certain people.
2. Do any of the policies and procedures indirectly discriminate against a particular group? An example would be performance criteria that would effectively exclude people who had responsibility for children.

checklist for your own institution

3. Do your policies and procedures have checks and balances to enable the identification of the operation of an individual's under-performance in terms of equal opportunities? For example if several people were involved in selection for promotion, do you have sufficient data to enable you to identify trends with individual selectors, so that if one of them was excluding say, women, you would be able to pick that up?
4. Do the stakeholders (the staff, managers, directors) in your institution have confidence in your policies and procedures and are there mechanisms for legitimate complaints and grievances to be made and mechanisms for such complaints and grievances to be properly investigated and dealt with?

Institutional discrimination – some applied examples

In this chapter, our discussions on institutional discrimination have largely focused on the issues arising from the Stephen Lawrence inquiry. This inquiry was primarily concerned with the impact of racial discrimination. But this book is not just about racism and we need to bear in mind that other people and groups of people may at times be on the receiving end of discrimination that arises out of the very nature of an institution or organization.

'built-in' discrimination

It is nearly always unintentional in the sense that it is not a deliberate published policy, but nevertheless has the effect of discriminating systematically against some sections of society. In some cases, this systematic discrimination is quite literally built in to the environment.

Pause for thought

Why do so many disabled people we meet tell us that it is not their disability that disables them but the environment in which they have to live?

If you are not a wheelchair user, imagine you are, and think of a regular journey you make; to work, the theatre, the gym, the shops or wherever. How would you do the journey if you were in a wheelchair? In your mind, start with your front door and go through the trip in detail.

If you are a wheelchair user, think about how you have to plan a trip. How easy is it to find out what you need to know? How often do you have to give up because it is just impossible? In your experience, have things got better or worse in respect of the built environment?

---

other examples

Other examples of institutionalized discrimination include the ban on gay men and women fostering or adopting children, policies adopted by social service agencies to prohibit what they term 'inter-racial' fostering, housing policies that place all members of ethnic minorities on the same housing estates and the poor provision of language support in schools for children for whom English is an additional language. Unfortunately, this list is only a tiny example of forms of institutional discrimination that exist at the moment.

Implications for personal and organizational growth

A professional quality organization or institution will always be on its guard against the problems of institutional discrimination that we have outlined in this chapter. Among the many working arrangements that may have to be examined for discriminatory bias, whether on the basis of ethnicity, gender, sexuality or disability, will be those for:

areas to examine

- recruitment;
- training;
- promotion;
- appraisal;
- allocation of roles, tasks and projects;
- working terms and conditions (including employment contracts and shift patterns);
- pay and other remuneration (including pension provisions and share options);
- transfer and relocation policies (including tenure policies);
- access to buildings and work areas;
- adjustments to working environments (Disability Discrimination Act 1995);
- provision of equipment and support material to staff;
- annual and other forms of leave (including maternity/paternity, sickness, compassionate and study leave);
- arrangements for part-time, job share and career break opportunities;
- access to goods and services offered or managed by the organization or institution;
- methods and policies of service delivery;
- complaints and grievance procedures (including the termination of employment procedures and policies).

You will notice from this list that some functions and arrangements are internal to an institution or organization and apply to the people that comprise its staff, whilst others relate to contact with customer or client. Irrespective of whether arrangements are internal or external, they need to be examined for their potential to create disadvantage or discrimination.

Implicit within the Macpherson definition are statements about potential goals of equal opportunities training, such as addressing attitudes as well as

the relevance to training

behaviour, raising awareness and raising levels of knowledge. An acceptance of institutional racism or discrimination can actually help to inform not only the goal of such training, but also its scope and content. Training should be inclusive of all members of an organization.

Each individual needs to be clear that they have a vital role to play in the eradication of discrimination within their own organization because each is bound up in the practices and procedures it follows. Not everybody makes policy or sets practice, but everybody has the power to question or challenge that policy or practice if they believe it to be discriminatory.

do I contribute to 'collective failure'?

'Collective failure' is a challenge to everyone in an institution or organization. It requires everyone to look within themselves at their own attitudes and behaviours, and outside themselves at the things they are required to do and the way they are required to do them. By doing this, they can identify ways in which they may be contributing to institutional discrimination. It takes courage to admit the possibility.

KEY POINTS IN THIS CHAPTER

- A major debate in equal opportunities in 1999 centred on the notion of institutional racism and institutional discrimination
- *The Macpherson Report* (published February 1999) identified a catalogue of errors in the police handling of the investigation into the death of Stephen Lawrence. Much of this was attributed to institutional racism. The report made 70 recommendations.
- Institutions were defined as sets of social practices and arrangements that shape and direct the way people within those institutions think and behave.
- The new definition of institutional discrimination provided by *The Macpherson Report* sets new standards for institutions and large organizations.
- The concept of institutional racism and/or discrimination has a number of consequences for organizations and individuals alike. These range from recruitment to morale.
- Institutional racism is not a phenomenon restricted to the police; examples may be drawn from education, housing and social service provision as well.

PERSONAL ACTION PLAN

Try answering the following questions:

How will the things I have learnt in this chapter change the way I think and act towards others who are different to me?

What has this chapter helped me to learn about myself with regard to:

- my beliefs;
- my attitudes;
- my values;
- my knowledge of others;
- my behaviour;
- my use of language;
- my responsibilities;
- the way I see the world?

How do I need to change in order to become:

- fairer;
- more sensitive;
- more understanding;
- less prejudicial;
- less discriminatory;
- more able to deal with people according to their needs?

If I were to change one thing about the way I act as a result of reading this chapter what would it be?

Chapter 9

Religion

After you have read this chapter we hope you will have a better knowledge of:

- why religion plays an important part in equal opportunities;
- the principal secular and religious festivals celebrated throughout the year;
- the main religions you will come across in this country and how you can be more sensitive to their followers; and
- systems for naming children which are used by certain religious groups.

WHY INCLUDE A CHAPTER ON RELIGION?

To some of you, it might seem strange to find a chapter about religion in a book on equal opportunities. But if you think about it, all religious groups in this country are minority groups, and as such they have the potential to be subjected to the same discrimination and unfairness as other minority groups. Indeed, in recent years there have been a number of equal opportunities cases which have had to do with the religious beliefs of the victim.

There are a number of other reasons why it is important to include some information about religions:

- Modern communications have led to the evolution of the idea of the global village. Events around the world are often reported live, and affect the way people here feel or behave. Such events often have their roots in religion. For example, the Gulf War of early 1991 has led to many false stereotypes about Muslims. In fact, in that war, this country fought alongside many Islamic states.
- Your own knowledge of the issues will help you better to understand why some things happen, and therefore to undertake your role with greater sensitivity to the people concerned.
- Religious beliefs are commonly very deeply held and as such are an area where ignorance of a person's belief or customs can often lead to offence. We have stressed throughout that treating people fairly can be partially achieved by being more sensitive to them as individuals. Greater under-

January

1st	New Year's Day (Gregorian Calendar)
1st–3rd	Oshogatu, New Year in Japan
6th	Twelfth Night
17th	Festival of St Anthony
21st Jan–20th Feb	Chinese New Year
25th	Burns Night
Late Jan–early Feb	Saraswati Puji, Hindu festival in India

February

2nd	TuB'Shvat, tree planting in Israel
2nd	Candlemas Day
3rd	Setsuban, start of spring in Japan
4th Feb–6th March	Festival of Lanterns
7th Feb–9th March	Mardi Gras/Carnival
Late Feb–March	Purim, Jewish festival
Late Feb–March	Shrove Tuesday/Pancake Day, beginning of Lent
Late Feb–March	Hola Mohalla, Sikh festival

March

1st	St David's Day in Wales
17th	St Patrick's Day in Ireland
22nd	Holi, Hindu New Year
Late March–April	Pesach, the Jewish Passover
Late March–April	Easter, Christian Good Friday and Easter Sunday

April

| 13th | Baisakhi, Sikh festival |
| 23rd | St George's Day in England |

May

1st	May Day
Late May–June	Wesak, Buddhist festival
Late May–June	Whitsun, Christian festival
Late May–June	Shavuot, Jewish festival

June

5th	Dragon Boat festival
c. 14th	Father's Day
21st	Midsummer's Day

July

4th	Independence day, USA
7th	Tanabata, Japanese star festival
15th	St Swithin's Day
July–Sept	Janmashtami, Hindu festival

August

| Early | Raksha Bandhan, Hindu festival |

September

1st–9th	Chinese Kite Festival
Early Sept	Ganesh's Birthday, Hindu festival
Mid-late	Rosh Hashana, Jewish festival
Mid-late	Yom Kippur, Jewish festival

October

c. 15th	Harvest Festivals
24th	United Nations Day
Late Oct–Nov	Diwali, Hindu festival of light
31st	Hallowe'en

November

2nd	All Souls' Day
5th	Guy Fawkes Night
15th	Shichogosan, Japanese feast day
Mid	Guru Nanak's, Sikh festival
Last Thursday	American Thanksgiving
30th	St Andrew's Day in Scotland

December

6th	Festival of St Nicholas
Mid	Hanukkah, Jewish festival of light
25th	Christmas Day
26th	Boxing Day, St Stephen's Day
31st	Hogmanay in Scotland

| Variable | Ramadan, Islamic holy month of fasting and abstinence |

Figure 9.1 *A selection of secular and religious festivals throughout the year*

standing of a person's religious belief and the strength with which they believe it is an essential ingredient of this.

- We argued earlier that one of the roots of prejudice is ignorance. For many of us, even a scant knowledge of the major world religions is lacking. In the sections that follow we hope you will at least be introduced to some of the major themes. Remember that, as always, you will be able to find exceptions to the rule. Our notes about the religions are brief and not intended to be all you would ever need to know. We do hope, however, that you will get the basic facts and that your interest in reading further will be stimulated.

A note on naming systems

If you are involved in a job which requires you to read or record names of other people you will know of the huge variety there are and that the same system for constructing them is not always followed. An understanding of the way names are made up is likely to improve both the efficiency of your recording, and the courtesy with which you do it. An obvious example of the courtesy issue would be that of asking Muslims, Jews, Hindus, Sikhs or Buddhists for their Christian name. They simply haven't got one! Several of the following sections contain information about the naming systems followed by that religion, with some examples of common names.

THE MAJOR RELIGIONS

All of the major religions celebrate festivals and have special times of religious significance. A knowledge of these will help you be more sensitive when others are celebrating or reflecting on their deeply held beliefs. Figure 9.1 gives a selection of festivals which you might come across. We have included some secular (non-religious) festivals as well to help put the others in context.

Buddhism

Founded about 2,500 years ago by Prince Siddhartha Gautama, who lived from about 463 to 483 BC in north-east India. He was known as Buddha, which means 'Awakened One'.

Concept of God

Buddhists do not believe in a creator God, nor do they worship gods. Their fundamental aim is to reach a state of Nirvana, or bliss, which is achieved through enlightenment and improvement through following the Eightfold Path (see below), with the help of Buddhist monks.

Holy writings

There are a number of sacred books called the Pali Canon, and a vast collection of sacred writings in Sanskrit, Tibetan and Chinese. One of these, 'The Way of Virtue' is learnt by heart by some Buddhists.

Major prophets

Gautama, the son of a north Indian ruler, was brought face to face with suffering and began looking for answers. Under the Tree of Enlightenment he found answers to the problem and became a Buddha, or Enlightened One. He expounded four noble truths:

- Suffering is a part of life.
- Suffering is caused by desire, or selfishness.
- Suffering will end if selfishness is destroyed.
- The way of destruction of suffering is the Eightfold Path. By following the Eightfold Path it is possible to reach the state of bliss known as Nirvana.

The Eightfold Path

Consists of:

- Right understanding: to see life as it is.
- Right thought: a pure mind, free from lust, ill-will or cruelty.
- Right action: no killing, stealing, adultery, but positive action: love, charity, generosity, honesty, etc.
- Right vocation: an occupation which harms no one.
- Right speech: free from falsehood, harshness, frivolity and slander.
- Right effort: prevent new evils and expel old ones, seek good and maintain existing good.
- Right mindfulness: concentrate to become aware of truth about the body, mind, feelings and thoughts.
- Right concentration: meditation to understand the impermanence of things.

Principal festivals

Central to the Buddhist celebration days are the anniversaries associated with their founder Gautama, his birth, enlightenment and death. Mahayana is the anniversary of the day on which Gautama became enlightened. Sakyamuni celebrates his birth, and Parinirvana the time when he slipped into a state of restfulness or bliss.

All three events, according to tradition, happened to fall in the lunar month of Vaisakha (April–May). This is the time for the festival known as

Wesak. In this three-day celebration buildings are decorated with flowers and lanterns, rows of candles are lit, and people gather for meditation in their homes and in the shrine rooms of the temples.

Places of worship

As noted above, Buddhists do not worship a god, but do have pagodas, stupas, or temples, which they may visit.

Practices and symbols

Buddhists may have a shrine in their home with a small image of the Buddha, and may sit crossed-legged before it whilst meditating. During times of festival, flowers are offered to the Buddha, presents are exchanged and gifts given to the poor.

Dietary needs

Buddhists are almost always vegetarian.

Christianity

Founded about 2,000 years ago by Jesus Christ, who lived from about 7 BC to AD 30. Since the Early Church of the first century there have been a number of branches of Christian tradition. The Eastern Orthodox Church is mainly represented by the Greek, Russian, Syrian, Armenian and Coptic churches. The western catholic tradition, which divided from the orthodox tradition, further split at the Reformation into Roman Catholics and Protestants. Protestants are mainly made up of the Lutheran, Reformed, Presbyterian, Pentecostal, Episcopal, Baptist, Methodist and other free churches.

Concept of God

God is a trinity of three persons in one: Father, Son (Jesus Christ), and Holy Spirit. In most (but not all) strands of Christianity they have equal, divine status.

Holy writings

The Bible (Old and New Testaments).

Major figures

Include such names as Moses, Isaiah and John the Baptist. The teachings of the apostles St Paul, St Peter and St John have been very influential in the development of Christianity.

Principal festivals

Christmas   The birth of Christ. With all the commercial trappings associated with Christmas, it has become almost a secular festival and much of the meaning which it has for Christians has become submerged.

Easter   Remembering the death and celebrating the resurrection of Jesus Christ. Good Friday and Easter Day occur during late March or early April. For many Christians Easter is the central festival of the Christian calendar, and takes the form of a joyous celebration of the new life of Jesus after his death on the cross. Whitsun, six weeks after Easter celebrates the coming of the Holy Spirit.

Practices and symbols

The symbol of the cross is particularly significant for Christians and in the last decade the ancient sign of the fish (originally used as a secret sign when Christians were facing persecution) has seen a resurgence. The letters in the Greek word for fish each stand in Greek for 'Jesus Christ Son of God, Saviour'.

   Holy communion, eucharist or mass is central to the worship of most Christians, and baptism, whether of infants or adults, is a feature of nearly all the Christian traditions and denominations.

Holy places

Many Christians regard some of the sacred sites in Israel, particularly Jerusalem, as being of special significance, such as the site of Jesus' crucifixion and resurrection.

Places of worship

Christians normally worship in church buildings, which can range in style and grandeur from St Paul's Cathedral, Westminster Abbey or Westminster Cathedral to much less grand structures, or even small halls in urban, suburban or rural areas. In recent years so-called 'house churches' have been growing up, and these often meet in places other than church buildings.

Dietary needs

Generally no dietary restrictions, although some Christians associate Friday with eating fish, and others impose self-restriction in terms of diet during the period of Lent (the six weeks leading up to Easter).

Naming systems

Generally speaking there is a strong link between religious background and names. There is a remnant of this in the use of the term 'Christian name', which relates principally to the name given to a child at baptism, and is often used even when the person does not claim any particular allegiance to Christianity. In fact, many Christian names are drawn from historical Judaism as well as from names developed after the time of Christ. David, for example, was the name of one of Israel's greatest kings.

Other features

- Most Christians find the use of the names Jesus and Christ as swear words to be very offensive.
- The basic philosophy of most Christians was summed up by Jesus in his teaching: 'Love the Lord your God with all your heart, and with all your soul and with all your strength; and love your neighbour as yourself.'

Hinduism

Hinduism is the name given by Europeans to the main, and most ancient, religion of the people of India. It has such a wide variety of practices and beliefs that the following information cannot do more than scratch the surface and indicate some of the more common features of the religion.

Concept of God

God is many deities. The supreme reality, called Brahman, is an impersonal being, neither male nor female. The three chief gods are Vishnu, the preserver, Shiva, the destroyer, and Brahma, the creator. Vishnu is often worshipped in the form of his incarnations, Krishna and Rama. The consort of Shiva, the great goddess Mahadevi, is often worshipped under many other names.

Holy writings

Bhagavad-Gita, the most popular and revered of the Hindu sacred books.

Major figures in Hinduism

Sri Ramakrishna (nineteenth century), Swami Vivekanada (Hindu reformer), both of whose birthdays are celebrated.

Principal festivals

The large number of gods involved in Hinduism means there are many festivals and celebrations.

Diwali   This is a festival of new year and new beginnings for the Hindu. It has light as a theme, representing the triumph of good over evil. Fireworks and extra lighting on houses are a feature of Diwali. The celebrations cover a five-day period.

Holi   A festival of celebration, singing and happiness, with street dancing, processions, and wearing bright clothes. Part of the celebration may include the spraying of coloured water or powder on one another. This recalls the traditional stories of when Lord Krishna's cowherds smeared red powder on each other. It's also just good fun!

Saravasti   Saravasti is the goddess of crafts, music and learning. At this festival she is worshipped by the placing of symbols of learning in front of her image. Prayers are particularly offered by those about to take examinations.

Practices and symbols

The practice of yoga has an important place in Hinduism. Through yoga, a person grows to understand the inner self by intensifying consciousness, and peace can be attained.

Holy places

The River Ganges in India has a particular significance for Hindus.

Places of worship

In India, Hindu temples are usually places where the priests serve the gods on behalf of the people, who make only occasional and individual visits to the temple. Daily worship is offered in the home, and only at times of festival do the temples become focal points of congregational worship.

Hindus in Western countries still worship mainly at home, but as a result of the stricter division of work and leisure time in such countries and the need for mutual support in an alien culture, more emphasis is placed on regular congregational worship in the temple. Hindu temples in the UK are generally converted buildings, sometimes houses. Before entering the place of worship, everyone must remove his/her shoes as a token of respect and to keep it clean.

Dietary needs

Hindus do not eat beef. Many will be vegetarian, and will not use tobacco or alcohol.

Hindu names

The basic pattern of names adopted by Hindus is given in Figure 9.2.

Personal name   This will be selected from a large number of possible names, and will normally be an indication of the sex of the person. As with most European names, personal names have a meaning.

Family name   In Hinduism, this is linked with the caste system, and the name gives information about the caste, or social position and occupation, of the owner. In India, the barriers created by the caste system are being slowly broken down, and as a result of this many Hindus have dropped the use of a caste name.

Recording   Because the family name is often not used, both the personal and the middle name should be obtained. It is preferable to record the family name if possible, but as noted above the person may be sensitive to its implications of status and caste and may refuse to give it.

Castes

Historically, Hindus have been identified with castes. The four castes were likened to parts of the body of Brahma: mouth, arms, thighs and feet. The highest caste was the Brahmana or priest, next the warrior caste, third the farmers, traders and artisans. The lowest caste did nothing other than serve the higher castes. The most unfortunate were those who belonged to no caste at all, namely 'the untouchables'. They were not allowed to enter villages and could not go into a temple. Mahatma Gandhi, in India, began to change attitudes towards castes and ensured that by law no person could be ascribed to such a group, and everyone had a right to enter the temples.

Islam

Founded about 1,400 years ago by the prophet Muhammad, who lived from about AD 570 to 632.

Concept of God

One God, whose name (in Arabic) is Allah.

Holy writings

Islam's holy writings are contained in the Quran, or Koran, the contents of which were revealed to Muhammad by the Angel Gabriel. Muhammad then recited the Quran, and it was written down by Arab scholars. Written originally in Arabic, it has been translated into many languages other than

Example of how a Hindu name might be made up

	Personal name	Complementary name	Family name
Female	Meena	Mayur	Shah
Male	Mayur	Bachulal	Shah

Personal names		Family names
Male	**Female**	
Anil	Aroti	Advani
Anoop	Aruna	Agarwal
Arun	Bakula	Aiyar
Bimal	Bimla	Anub
Binoy	Bindoo	Ashar
Devendra	Charulata	Chauhan
Dinesh	Ela	Chopra
Gopal	Gayatri	Dar
Govind	Indira	Desai
Jayant	Jayashree	Gupta
Jayesh	Leela	Iyer
Kanti	Leena	Kazi
Kapil	Lopa	Kulkarni
Krishna	Majula	Lalwani
Madhav	Meena	Modi
Mauur	Mira	More
Naresh	Mohini	Naidoo
Nuranjan	Mukhta	Patel
Niarmal	Nirupa	Prabhu
Rajendra	Nandita	Pradhan
Rajesh	Psehpa	Yaji
Ram	Rupa	Ramgovind
Ravi	Sandya	Roy
Sumant	Tara	Shah
Suresh	Vishni	Sharma
Vijay		Shenoy
		Varty

Figure 9.2 *A selection of Hindu names, and how they are constructed*

Arabic, but of course, as with any translation, the original text is to be preferred.

Major prophets

A succession of prophets from the beginning of time, from Abraham and Moses, through Mary and Jesus to Muhammad in the seventh century. It is customary for a Muslim to say 'May peace be upon him!' when Muhammad's name is mentioned.

Principal festivals and practices

Faithful observance of the faith is supported on the Five Pillars of Islam. These are:

The declaration of faith   'I bear witness that there is no god but Allah, and I bear witness that Muhammad is his servant and messenger.'

The five daily prayers   These are prayers to Allah, and the times are usually between dawn and sunrise, after midday, mid-afternoon, just after sunset and the early part of the night.

Fasting during the month of Ramadan   To keep strictly to the fast, Muslims will abstain from food, drink and sexual intercourse from dawn until sunset. During this holy month, it is equally important for the Muslim to abstain from all evil and malicious thoughts. Ramadan concludes with a festival known as Eid al-Fitr (pronounced eed al fitter), the festival of fast-breaking. It starts on the first day of the following month and is an occasion of joy and celebration extending over three days.

Giving relief to the poor   This practice is known as Zakat. Generally 2.5 per cent of net wealth is given annually in support of the less well off.

The pilgrimage to Mecca   This should be undertaken at least once in a lifetime, provided one has the necessary financial means.

Another major festival is Eid al-Adha (the festival of sacrifice), which is celebrated over four days. It occurs after the time of the pilgrimage to Mecca (regardless of whether the pilgrimage has actually been made). An animal will be sacrificed according to a holy ritual and the meat divided into three, one part for the family, one for the person sacrificing and one part to be given to the poor. In this country, the sacrificing is only done at licensed slaughterhouses where the animal will be killed according to Islamic tradition.

Holy places

Mecca, in Saudi Arabia, is the principal holy place. It was the place of the prophet Muhammad's birth in AD 570.

Places of worship

Muslims meet for congregational worship in mosques (from the Arabic *masjid*, literally 'place of prostration'). Mosques may also be places of education and teaching. Public worship at a mosque on a Friday will normally include a sermon. Mosques are to be found throughout Britain, and in London one of the most strikingly beautiful examples is the Regents Park mosque with its enormous bronze-coloured dome. Shoes are removed before entering a mosque.

Dietary needs

Muslims do not eat pork or any other meat which has not been ritually slaughtered. Meat which has been through the process of ritual slaughter is known as halal meat.

Islamic names

There are no strict rules to be observed in naming a child. Many personal or first names, however, are those of the prophets mentioned in the Quran (see Figure 9.3).

Other features

- The word Islam means peace and submission.
- Recent world events have caused Islam to be misrepresented in the minds of some people. In fact, its teaching strongly emphasizes the brotherhood of mankind, and sets the tone for Muslims' relationships with others. Examples of this teaching are found in the Hadith literature, which helps to explain the teaching of the Quran. Two examples are: 'All creatures are God's children, and those dearest to God are the ones who treat his children kindly' (Hadith). 'He from whose injurious conduct his neighbour is not safe will not enter Paradise' (Hadith).
- Muslims form two distinct groups: the Sunna or Sunni Muslims and the Shia or Shiite Muslims. The former account for about 80 per cent of the Muslims of the world. The Shia are mainly concentrated in Iran, Iraq, Pakistan, India, the Yemen and East Africa.
- Most Muslim boys are circumcised.
- The Islamic holy day of the week is Friday.
- Muslim religious leaders are called imams.

Males			Females
Abbas	Hafeez	Mukhtar	Asmat
Abdul	Halim	Muzzamil	Azara
Afsal	Hanif	Qasim	Ayesha
Akbar	Hasan	Rafiq	Fatima
Akram	Hashim	Rahman	Ismat
Ali	Haq	Rashid	Jameelar
Alam	Hussaim	Sadiq	Kulsum
Amin	Ibrahim	Salim	Najma
Araf	Ifthikar	Samsur	Naseema
Ashaf	Iqbal	Shaif	Nasreen
Aslam	Ismael	Sharif	Nasrat
Azam	Jafar	Sulaiman	Parveen
Aziz	Khaliq	Sultan	Rabia
Badar	Latif	Umar	Razwana
Badhur	Mahoud	Usman	Savera
Bashir	Malik	Yaqub	Sadaqat
Farrukh	Massur	Yousaf	Salma
Ghafar	Masud	Yousif	Sughra
Ghulam	Mir	Yusuf	Surriya
Gulab	Miraj	Zahid	Zubaida
Habib	Mubashir		

Figure 9.3   *Some common Islamic personal names*

Judaism

Founded about 4,000 years ago by the Hebrew chieftain Abraham, who taught his people to worship one God – Jehovah or Yahweh.

Concept of God

One God whose name is so holy it cannot be uttered. God is referred to by the name Adoni.

Holy writings

Chief writings are contained in the Torah, which reveals the will of God, and the Talmud, which contains Jewish religious and civil laws. The Torah is made up of the first five books of the Old Testament: Genesis, Exodus, Leviticus, Numbers and Deuteronomy.

Major figure

Moses, the one to whom the Law was given on Mount Sinai.

Principal festivals

New Year   The Jewish calendar is based on cycles of the moon. The Jewish new year occurs in September or October and is the first major festival. There are no parallels with the revelling of non-religious new year celebrations. Rather it is a special day of prayer, marking the beginning of ten days of penitence.

Day of Atonement   The ten days (above) end with the most solemn day in the Jewish calendar – the Day of Atonement, known as Yom Kippur, a day of fasting. The day is spent in prayer in the synagogue. The fast lasts for 24 hours from sunset on the previous day.

Sukkot   About one week after Yom Kippur is the Jewish equivalent of the harvest festival, known as Sukkot, when families build a booth outside their houses or synagogues, made with branches and leaves and decorated with fruit and flowers.

Channukah   Pronounced 'hannaka', this is the festival of lights to commemorate the rebuilding of the Temple in biblical times. The festival lasts for a week and each night, candles are lit on a nine-branch candelabra, known as a *menorah*. The festival starts with two candles and by the last night all nine are lit. The first candle is used to light the others.

Passover   Celebration of the time when the angel of death passed over the Jewish households during the captivity in Egypt, and their subsequent freedom.

Clothing

It is traditional for men to cover their heads when in the synagogue or at a cemetery. Additionally, all devout Jewish men and boys will wear a hat of some description, including a skullcap. Most of Britain's Jewish people are indistinguishable from non-Jews in the way they dress. There is one particularly distinctive group, however, the Hassidim. They wear clothing of dark colours only. The men wear wide-brimmed hats and long coats. They grow their hair long, and plait the sideburns.

Dietary laws

The extent to which these are upheld will depend on the individual, and the extent of their orthodoxy. Here are some of the more common laws:

Jews are forbidden to eat any animal which does not chew the cud and has a cloven hoof (principally pigs). Shellfish is also forbidden. Many Jews will not mix dairy produce with meat; this may extend to using separate crockery, and cooking utensils for milk and meat.

'Kosher' means that food has been prepared in accordance with all the dietary laws. In the case of meat, for example, it means that it has been slaughtered in a way which allows all the animal's blood to drain away. In the case of other food which might contain animal or fish products, there must have been no contact with banned items. Because so many Jews in this country came originally from Eastern Europe, traditional meals tend to reflect the food from that area. Salt beef, bagels, goulash, and borsch (thick soup) are all examples. In any area where there is a high density of Jewish people, you will find a number of Kosher food shops including butchers and delicatessens. You may also find Kosher food counters in some larger supermarkets.

Holy places

Israel as a whole has a special significance for Jewish people.

Places of worship

The Jewish building of worship is the synagogue. The word 'synagogue' means 'to gather together'. It is the centre of Jewish activity, being a place for prayer and meeting others, a school and a centre of administration.

Other features

- Bar Mitzvah is a ceremony which occurs at the age of 13, when a boy becomes a 'son of the law'. More recently, in some traditions, a similar ceremony, known as a Bat Mitzvah, has been introduced for girls.
- Jewish male babies are circumcised eight days after birth. This is a religious requirement and a religious ceremony is usually held, although the operation is performed by a medically qualified person.
- The religious leader is known as a rabbi (literally 'teacher'). Over the years rabbis have interpreted and commented on the Law as given to Moses and this has been handed down in what are known as Rabbinical writings.
- The Sabbath is celebrated from sunset on Friday to sunset on Saturday. In addition, devout Jews may attend prayers three times daily throughout the week.

Sikhism

Founded in India in about AD 1500 by Guru Nanak who lived from 1469 to 1539 and was the first of ten gurus (teachers) of the Sikh religion.

Concept of God

One God; a great, merciful and loving creator whose spirit pervades all creation. There is no distinction between the spiritual and the material.

Holy writings

Adi Granth, also referred to as the Holy Guru Granth and the Guru Granth Sahib (see below).

Major prophets

There were ten great gurus (guru means spiritual teacher). Guru Nanak (1469–1539) was the first and greatest of the gurus and founded the Sikh religion in the fifteenth century. He was followed by nine other gurus spanning 240 years (1469–1708). Guru Arjan (1563–1606) was the fifth guru. He compiled a collection of his own and his predecessors' poems and hymns, called the Adi Granth (which means the First Collection).

Guru Gobind Singh was the last guru.

- He founded the brotherhood of Sikhs, the Khalsa (which means the pure ones). This is an inner circle of Sikh men and women who have been fully initiated into the faith by baptism (Amrit), and who uphold the five signs of the brotherhood, the five Ks (see below).
- He added further hymns to the Adi Granth and gave it its final and complete form.

Principal festivals

Baisakhi   The most important of the Sikh festivals, which occurs on or around 13 April. It commemorates the day in 1699 when Guru Gobind Singh called for a volunteer to give his life for the faith. One volunteered and went into a tent with the guru, who later emerged with a bloodstained sword. Four others did the same and then it was revealed that the five volunteers were unhurt and alive. They became known as the Khalsa, which means pure ones, and they were the first of the Sikh brotherhood.

Diwali   A very similar festival to that of the Hindus, and celebrated in much the same way. It centres on a theme of light and joy, and celebrates the release of the sixth guru, Hargobind, from captivity. The Golden Temple at Amritsar is lavishly decorated with illuminations.

Hola Mohalla   The spring festival, which lasts about three days.

Gurpurbs   Birthdays and martyrdom days of the gurus.

Practices and symbols

The five signs of the brotherhood – the five Ks, which Guru Gobind Singh required his followers to wear on their bodies at all times until their death. These are:

Kesh (uncut hair)   This includes beards for males. Kesh is the chief emblem of a Sikh man or woman. Hair on the body is God-given and as such is worn as a symbol of faith, truth and the highest qualities of the mind.

Kanga (comb)   Closely linked with Kesh, and symbolizes that the hair should be kept clean and healthy. It is used to keep the hair in place and is also a symbol to remind the wearer to keep his or her mind under control also.

Kirpan (sword)   Usually worn as a small replica of a sword. Its purpose is summed up in the words of Guru Gobind Singh: 'When all other names fail to curb tyranny, it is right to wield the sword.' Sikh thinking, however, stresses that the mind is important and that every man is to have a mind like a sword, expressing hope and spiritual radiance.

Kacherra (shorts)   A symbol of chastity (sexual relationships are only to be within the context of marriage) and readiness, enables brisk movement in time of action.

Kara (steel bangle)   Always made of steel and a reminder to the wearer that he or she is bound both morally and spiritually to the teaching of the Guru.

Holy places

The Golden Temple at Amritsar has a special significance.

Places of worship

Sikh temples or *gurdwara* are the focus for public worship. Regardless of the grandeur of the building, there will be a central place for the Guru Granth Sahib (holy book), which will be enthroned on a dais underneath a decorative canopy.

Dietary needs

Sikhs do not eat halal meat and will not eat beef. Many Sikhs are vegetarians.

Sikh names (see Figure 9.4).

The name Singh means 'lion', and is used by all Sikh males. Kaur (pronounced 'core'), which means 'princess', is used by Sikh women.

Personal names		Family (subcaste) names	
Ajit	Mohinder	Areehal	Manku
Amarjit	Paramjit	Bahra	Mathara
Baljit	Piara	Bassi	Pannesar
Daljit	Pritam	Bhambra	Phull
Davindar	Rajinder	Birdi	Purewal
Dibag	Ramindar	Brar	Ryat
Gurmit	Ranjit	Chana	Sambhi
Harbans	Ravinder	Dhanjal	Sandhu
Joginder	Sewa (male)	Dhesi	Sidhu
Kuldip	Sohan	Gill	Sohanpaul
Malkiat	Surjit	Grewal	Sonal
Manjit	Swaran	Kalsi	Thandi
Mohan		Man	

Figure 9.4   *A selection of Sikh personal and family names*

Family name   This may well indicate a place of origin or caste and is often dropped by the owner. In fact, the adoption of Singh and Kaur for many Sikhs is a positive assertion of their religious identity and rejection of the inequality implicit in castes. This means that you might well have to explain why you would prefer to take a record of a name which will help to distinguish the person from other Singhs or Kaurs. Most Sikhs readily accept the need to reveal their family name, but you should, of course, respect the person's reasons for not wishing to reveal it.

Titles   There are some equivalents to the European conventions: Mr approximates to 'Sirdar'; Mrs approximates to 'Sirdani'; and Miss approximates to 'Bibi'.

Other features

- The Sikh community in Southall, London represents the largest concentration of Sikhs outside the Indian sub-continent.
- Sikhism forbids its followers certain things, including smoking, using intoxicants, taking drugs (except on the advice of a doctor). It also prohibits adultery of any nature, even in a dream.

PERSONAL ACTION PLAN

Try answering the following questions:

How will the things I have learnt in this chapter change the way I think and act towards others who are different to me?

What has this chapter helped me to learn about myself with regard to:

- my beliefs;
- my attitudes;
- my values;
- my knowledge of others;
- my behaviour;
- my use of language;
- my responsibilities;
- the way I see the world?

How do I need to change in order to become:

- fairer;
- more sensitive;
- more understanding;
- less prejudicial;
- less discriminatory;
- better able to deal with people according to their needs?

If I were to change one thing about the way I act as a result of reading this chapter what would it be?

Chapter 10

Equal Opportunities Law, Agencies and Links to Further Information

In this final chapter we have included information and references that will allow you to follow up the themes raised in other parts of the book. It has been written as an A–Z of the law relating to equal opportunities and some of the agencies designed to promote these laws.

By the time you have read through this chapter, we hope you will have:

- a better idea of some of the more important aspects of the legislation designed to promote equal opportunities; and
- a working knowledge of some of the statutory bodies and agencies who are involved in promoting equal opportunities in this country.

INTRODUCTION

The law relating to equal opportunities is fairly extensive and in some places quite complicated. We have arranged the principal aspects of it into an A–Z format for two main reasons. First, there is some overlap between law aimed at different problems, as is the case with sex and race discrimination. Second, legislation is not always very accessible, and we hope that in this A–Z format you will find your way around more easily.

We do just need to mention what this chapter is not intended to be. It is not a glossary of terms relating to equal opportunities. Where we have come across jargon in the text we have tried to highlight and explain it.

To explain specific sections of the legislation we have used examples from the real world. The examples we have chosen are intended to highlight how things relate to you personally rather than to the duties of employers. If you are an employer you will need to seek more comprehensive information on your specific responsibilities. The Commission for Racial Equality and the Equal Opportunities Commission are both statutory bodies which would be a good starting point. You will find more information about them in the A–Z.

Where you see this symbol ☞ we have included the Internet address of a related Web site. The Internet is a powerful reference source for a great deal of information about equal opportunities including the full text of legislation.

Finally, the problem with an A–Z is what to include and what to leave out. As far as supportive agencies are concerned, we have included the mainstream ones who have a particular interest in the four main issues we have dealt with, namely sexism, racism, disability and sexuality. Our inclusions are not exhaustive, and generally represent only those we have come across either directly or in our reading. We welcome suggestions through the publisher for further inclusions.

A–Z OF LAWS, AGENCIES AND LINKS TO FURTHER INFORMATION

Access courses

As their name suggests, access courses are designed to provide training, advice and support that enables people from minority groups to gain access to employment or education opportunities at an equal level to everyone else. The training and guidance offered aims to offset the effects of discrimination suffered by such groups and their members in other parts of the social system, particularly education. They may offer help in such areas as numeracy, literacy, language skills, self-confidence and assertiveness, as well as specific training in interviewing techniques and selection processes. (See also **positive action**.)

Action for Blind People

A national UK charity which aims to enable blind and partially sighted people to enjoy equal opportunities in every aspect of their lives through work, leisure, housing and support.

14–16 Verney Road
London
SE16 3DZ

☞ www.vois.org.uk/afbp/

Advisory Conciliation and Arbitration Service (ACAS)

This body, much more commonly referred to by its acronym ACAS, is charged with the duty of trying to resolve disputes arising out of employment-related issues before they get as far as an industrial tribunal. In most cases, copies of documents are sent to a conciliation officer from ACAS, who will help the parties to try to reach a settlement. There is no compulsion on the parties in a dispute to speak to ACAS.

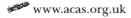 www.acas.org.uk

Amnesty International

Amnesty International is a worldwide campaigning movement that works to promote all the human rights enshrined in the **Universal Declaration of Human Rights** (see below) and other international standards. Amnesty International campaigns to free all prisoners of conscience, ensure fair and prompt trials for political prisoners, abolish the death penalty, torture and other cruel treatment of prisoners, end political killings and 'disappearances' and oppose human rights abuses by opposition groups.

 www.amnesty.org

Commission for Racial Equality (CRE)

The Commission for Racial Equality (CRE) was provided for by the Race Relations Act 1976. Section 43(1) of the Act sets out the duties of the Commission:

- To work towards the elimination of discrimination.
- To promote equality of opportunity and good relations between persons of different racial groups generally.
- To keep under review the working of the Act, and when required by the Secretary of State, or when it otherwise thinks it necessary, to draw up and submit to the Secretary of State proposals for amending it.

As part of its function the CRE supplies information about the working of the Race Relations Act. An excellent guide to its functions, and various types of statistical information relating to equal opportunities, can be found in its annual report, which is available from the Commission for a small charge.

Commission for Racial Equality
Head office
10–12 Allington Street
London
SW1E 5EH

The CRE also has offices in Edinburgh, Manchester, Leeds and Leicester.

 www.cre.gov.uk

Criminal Justice and Public Order Act 1994

This Act introduces a new class of criminal offences classified as racially aggravated offences. The effect of this legislation is to make it clear to the courts where an offence is motivated or aggravated by racism.

> 28(1) An offence is racially aggravated for the purposes of sections 29 to 32 of The Criminal Justice and Public Order Act 1994 below if:
>
> (a) at the time of committing the offence, or immediately before or after doing so, the offender demonstrates towards the victim of the offence hostility based on the victim's membership (or presumed membership) of a racial group; or
> (b) the offence is motivated (wholly or partly) by hostility towards members of a racial group based on their membership of that group.

Persons convicted of racially aggravated offences face increased punishment because of the extra racial dimension of their crime.

Additionally the Act provides for an offence of racial harassment, which covers harassment of a tenant by a landlord, and harassment of an employee by an employer.

If you think you have been the victim of a racially aggravated offence you should seek advice, guidance and support from the police. Where you feel that you have been harassed by your landlord or employer based upon your ethnicity you should seek help and advice from a solicitor, a racial equality council or from a citizens advice bureau. You will find details of your local facilities at your local library, town hall, police station or in your local telephone book.

 www.hmso.gov.uk/acts.htm

Daycare Trust

The national childcare charity working to promote high quality affordable childcare for all. Advises childcare providers, employers, trade unions and policymakers on childcare.

Daycare Trust
Shoreditch Town Hall Annexe
380 Old Street
London
EC1V 9LT

Helpline: 020 7739 2866

 www.daycaretrust.org.uk

Direct discrimination

The overlap between the two main pieces of anti-discrimination legislation (the Race Relations Act 1976 and the Sex Discrimination Act 1975) is such that they are best dealt with together.

Direct race discrimination

This occurs when a person is treated less favourably than another, on grounds of colour, race, nationality, or ethnic or national origins. For employment issues the scope of the law includes:

- terms of employment;
- access to opportunities for promotion, training, transfer, or any other benefits, facilities or services; and
- dismissal or subjecting the person to any other detriment (detriment means anything which disadvantages the person).

It would therefore be unlawful direct discrimination to refuse, on racial grounds, to employ a person, or to deny suitably qualified candidates an interview. A practical example of this would be the case of a firm refusing to employ a black person as a receptionist because they might discourage customers.

The scope of the Acts also covers housing, education and services. Some selected examples of what is covered include:

- *Housing.* Anyone selling property or letting rented accommodation discriminating against a would-be buyer or tenant; landlords or other managers of property who unlawfully discriminate against any occupier of that property.
- *Education.* Educational institutions refusing or deliberately omitting to admit an applicant on grounds of race, or varying the terms of admission or the way it provides benefits, facilities or services to its pupils or students. There are two exceptions to this: where an institution might be allowed to discriminate in relation to the education or training of persons normally resident overseas, or to meet the needs of particular racial groups, for example special language classes.
- *Public houses, shops, restaurants, places of entertainment, etc.* In all these cases it would be unlawful to discriminate on racial grounds by refusing entry, refusing service, offering less favourable terms, or providing an inferior service. As an example, it would be unlawful discrimination for a public house to display a 'No gypsies' sign on the door.
- *Obtaining goods, facilities, or other services.* Selected examples of what the Act would encompass include insurance companies, banks, building societies, doctors, solicitors, local authorities and many more. Again, it is unlawful for any of these to refuse to provide their goods or service,

make their terms less favourable or offer an inferior service on racial grounds.

Direct sex discrimination

This means being treated less favourably than a person of the opposite sex is (or would be) treated in similar circumstances. Direct discrimination on the basis of sex often shows itself as a manifestation of traditional stereotypes about the roles of men and women, and what might be considered 'men's jobs' or 'women's jobs'. An example would be where a woman was not selected for a job involving danger, such as in the construction industry, because it was felt that it was inappropriate for her, as a woman, to be in dangerous situations. A decision not to select a woman in these circumstances would amount to direct unlawful sex discrimination.

As with racial discrimination the scope of the law includes:

- employment;
- education;
- housing, goods, facilities and services; and
- advertising.

Direct marriage discrimination

This means being treated less favourably than an unmarried person of the same sex is (or would be) treated in similar circumstances. An example would be refusing to employ a woman in a post which required long-term training because she was married and might want to leave to have children.

If a woman was asked the following questions at a selection interview either for a job, or for promotion or transfer within employment, it would probably indicate that unlawful direct marriage discrimination was taking place:

- 'Do you have any intention of getting married?'
- 'Do you have any plans for a family?'
- 'How would your husband feel about you doing this kind of work?'
- 'Do you think your family ties will get in the way of your doing this job effectively?'

With selection interviews, a good general rule of thumb to test whether or not the questions being asked are valid is to establish whether the same questions are being put to both men and women, and whether the question can be justified as being genuine requirements for the job (see **genuine occupational qualifications** below).

www.hmso.gov.uk/acts.htm

Disability Discrimination Act 1995

This important new law has been introduced to combat prejudice and discrimination against disabled persons and to make it easier for them to get or remain in work. In addition, it sets out to improve access for them to buildings, transport and services.

The Act has provided for the creation of a National Disability Council to advise the Government on ways in which prejudice and discrimination against disabled persons can be minimized or even eliminated altogether.

Another important part of the Act is a new duty on employers to improve the working environments in which disabled staff work in order to overcome disadvantages arising from the way the workplace is set out or the work arranged.

These improvements include:

- making adjustments to premises;
- allocating some of the disabled person's duties to another person;
- transferring the person to fill an existing vacancy;
- altering the person's working hours;
- assigning the person to a different place of work;
- allowing the person to be absent during working hours for rehabilitation, assessment or treatment;
- giving the person, or arranging for the person to be given, training;
- acquiring or modifying equipment;
- modifying instructions or reference manuals;
- modifying procedures for testing or assessment;
- providing a reader or interpreter;
- providing supervision.

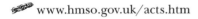 www.hmso.gov.uk/acts.htm

Disabled Persons Act 1981

The 1981 Act places a duty on the providers of buildings and premises to comply with standards of access for people with a disability, and also places a duty on highway authorities to have regard for the needs of blind and disabled persons.

www.hmso.gov.uk/acts.htm   www.disability.gov.uk

Equal Pay Act 1970 and Equal Pay (Amendment) Act 1983

Both these pieces of legislation are aimed at eliminating discrimination between men and women in terms of payment for equal work and contractual conditions. The 1983 legislation brought Britain into line with the European directive on equal pay for equal work.

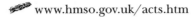 www.hmso.gov.uk/acts.htm

Equal Opportunities Commission (EOC)

The Equal Opportunities Commission was set up by Parliament in 1975. Its three main objectives are to:

- enforce the laws created by Parliament to eliminate unlawful sex discrimination;
- promote equality of opportunity generally between women and men;
- review and propose amendments to the existing legislation.

At the time of writing the main focus of the work of the EOC is:

- to improve access to justice;
- the establishment of a safe and harassment-free working environment;
- equalization of pension rights, without detriment to the rights of women;
- non-discriminatory payment and job evaluation systems;
- successful combination of working life with family commitments;
- satisfactory rights for part-time workers;
- a totally independent tax structure for husbands and wives. (*Source:* EOC, 1993.)

Equal Opportunities Commission (EOC)
Overseas House
Quay Street
Manchester
M3 3HN

The EOC also has offices in Glasgow and Cardiff.

 www.eoc.org.uk

Equal opportunities policies

In recent years, equal opportunities policies have flourished, and most larger organizations now have a policy of one form or another. You can see evidence of this in many job adverts in the local and national press. You will frequently see the words 'committed to equal opportunities' or 'working for equal opportunities' at the foot of adverts, or in some cases potted versions of the organization's policy will appear.

We do need to be careful not to be too naïve about equal opportunities policies. It is all too easy to fall into an attitude of 'do as I say' rather than 'do as I do'. What we mean is that the mere existence of an equal opportunities policy proves nothing other than the ability of the organization to write and publish a policy. To be effective it will need bite, and this in our experience will mean (not in any particular order):

- Overt management commitment to it, evidenced by sincere behaviour and attitudes.
- A commitment to training staff, raising their awareness and increasing their sensitivity to the issues. This commitment will often be evidenced by a willingness to provide the necessary resources.
- Internal monitoring systems to assess progress.
- Systems and procedures to permit staff to complain if they feel they are being treated unfairly. It is vital that the staff have faith in the effectiveness of the system and the sincerity of those who will operate it.

In its booklet (EOC, 1986) the Equal Opportunities Commission gives further advice about the components of equal opportunities policies. In summary, they are:

- definitions of direct and indirect discrimination;
- the organization's commitment to equal opportunities;
- names of those responsible for implementation;
- details of implementation structures;
- the obligation on employees to comply;
- procedures for dealing with complaints;
- examples of what is unacceptable;
- details of arrangements for monitoring; and
- a commitment to the removal of barriers to equal opportunity within the organization.

 www.eoc.org.uk

European Convention on Human Rights

The Convention was drafted in the 1950s and provides rights to individuals against actions of the state and authorities acting for the state. The mechanism by which the rights enshrined in the Convention could be enforced was in the form of the European Commission on Human Rights and the European Court of Human Rights. The **Human Rights Act 1998** (see entry in this A–Z) provides a domestic remedy for those who claim their rights under the European Convention have been violated. The main Convention articles and protocols covered are summarized below. They are intended to give you a flavour of what is included and do not contain the definitive wording. Refer to the Convention and the Human Rights Act 1998 for full details.

Article 2 Right to life protected by law;

Article 3 No torture, inhuman or degrading treatment or punishment;

Article 4 No slavery, servitude or forced labour;

Article 5 Liberty and security of the person apart from lawful arrest and detention;

Article 6 Fair and public hearing of charges within a reasonable time; innocent until proven guilty;

Article 7 No retrospective guilt for an act which was not a crime at the time it was committed;

Article 8 Right to respect for private life, home and correspondence;

Article 9 Freedom of thought, conscience and religion;

Article 10 Freedom of expression (limited only by duties and responsibilities);

Article 11 Freedom of peaceful assembly;

Article 12 Rights to marry and found a family;

Article 14 Rights and freedoms in the convention to be enjoyed without discrimination on any ground such as sex, race, colour, language, religion, political or other opinion, national or social origin, association with a national minority, property, birth or other status.

First Protocol

Article 1 Peaceful enjoyment of possessions;

Article 2 The right to education;

Article 3 Free elections by secret ballot.

www.pfc.org.uk/legal/hra98b.htm

www.europa.eu.int/index.htm

www.europa.eu.int/abc/cit1.eu.htm

Genuine occupational qualifications

There are a limited number of circumstances where discrimination may be allowed on the basis of race or sex and these are known as genuine occupational qualifications. In terms of the Race Relations Act, an example would be where the holder of a particular job has responsibility for providing for the welfare of a particular racial group, and that can be most effectively done by a member of the same group. A practical example of this would be a job advertisement by the National Society for the Prevention of Cruelty to Children for a 'Black Family Care Worker' where the advert makes it clear that it is claiming exemption, under section 5(2)d of the Act, and the post-holder needs to be black (*Nursery World*, 14 October 1993).

In the same way there are a limited number of jobs which have the gender of the post-holder as a genuine occupational qualification. For example, an advertising agency would be within the law to specify that they were looking for males only to model a new range in men's underwear. Roles for actors are another area where there may be a genuine occupational qualification on the basis of gender. However, the limited scope of genuine occupational qualifications means that in the vast majority of cases, it is not lawful to advertise jobs for 'men' or 'women' only.

 www.eoc.org.uk

Government Disability Website

The Government Disability Website provides various online information about government initiatives and policies that impact on people with disability. It includes comprehensive information on the Disability Discrimination Act and offers advice about the act for employers, employees and job-seekers.

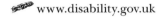 www.disability.gov.uk

Home Office Race Equality Unit

The Unit is responsible for race relations policy and legislation and helps promote equal opportunities in other Home Office policy areas and in outside agencies.

Home Office Race Equality Unit
Home Office
Queen Anne's Gate
London
SW1

 www.homeoffice.gov.uk/reu/reu.htm

Human Rights Act 1998

The Human Rights Act is designed to give further effect to the rights and freedoms guaranteed under the European Convention on Human Rights. This means that it is unlawful for a public authority to act in a way which is incompatible with a Convention right (Section 6(1)). 'Public authority' includes courts and tribunals and any person whose functions are functions of a public nature (Section 6(3)). Proceedings may now be brought in *this* country by someone who claims that a public authority has acted in contravention of one of the Convention rights covered by the Act. To see the full scope of the Human Rights Act you can refer to the summary of the European Convention rights in this A–Z. Also, use the web-link to see the full text of the Act.

 www.pfc.org.uk/legal/hra98b.htm

Indirect discrimination

Indirect racial discrimination

Consists of applying, in any circumstances covered by the Act, a requirement or condition which, although applying equally to persons of all racial groups, is such that a considerably smaller proportion of a particular racial group can comply with it, and it cannot be shown to be justifiable on anything other than racial grounds.

For example, to impose a height limit of five feet ten inches as a condition for people wishing to apply for a particular occupation would effectively exclude many whose ethnic origins were from the Indian sub-continent and South East Asia, where the average height is below that of white males in this country. Police forces and the prison service are, in fact, specifically allowed to discriminate on grounds of height, but many have waived this right to try and remove at least one of the barriers to a fair representation of the communities they serve.

Indirect sex discrimination

This is more difficult to establish. It means being unable to comply with a requirement or condition which, on the face of it, applies equally to men and women, but which, in practice, can be met by far fewer people of one sex than the other. Such a requirement or condition is lawful only if it can be objectively justified.

A good example of indirect sex discrimination is given in a recent article by Peter Vallely (1993) who suggests that although women account for more than half of the population (the 1991 census showed 51.6 per cent), there are six million fewer female than male drivers in this country. If a job did not *depend* on the employee holding a driving licence, but nevertheless made that a condition, as a useful additional qualification, then the effect would be to indirectly disadvantage a larger group of women than men.

Indirect marriage discrimination

This works in a similar way. It means being unable to comply with a requirement or condition which, on the face of it, applies equally to married and single people, but which in practice, can be met by far fewer married people than single people. Such a requirement is only lawful if it is objectively justifiable.

 www.cre.gov.uk   www.eoc.org.uk

Industrial tribunals

These are independent judicial bodies, made up of a legally qualified chairperson and two other members who are drawn from two panels of members appointed by the Secretary of State for Employment. Both employers and employees' organizations are consulted about the appointment of these members. They were set up to provide a less formal way of settling disputes between employers and employees. There are permanent offices in the larger centres of population and tribunals sit in most parts of the country. The principal matters which may be considered by industrial tribunals include:

- equal pay;
- maternity rights;
- occupational pension schemes;
- race relations;
- redundancy;
- sex discrimination;
- trade union membership and non-membership rights;
- the right to receive written reasons for dismissal; and
- the right to receive a written statement of terms of employment.

You should be aware that there are strict time limits on the registration of cases with industrial tribunals. These limits depend on the type of case being brought.

www.dti.gov.uk/index.htm   www.dti.gov.uk/pip/23intri.htm

Institute of Race Relations (IRR)

The London-based Institute of Race Relations (IRR) conducts research and produces educational resources which are at the cutting edge of the struggle for racial justice in Britain and internationally. It seeks to reflect the experience of those who suffer racial oppression and draws its perspectives from the most vulnerable in society.

Institute of Race Relations
2–6 Leeke Street
King's Cross Road
London
WC1X 9HS
Tel: 020 7833 2010
Tel: 020 7837 0041

www.homebeats.co.uk

Institutional Discrimination (including institutional racism and sexism)

Chapter 8 covers this important subject in great detail. This chapter provides an explanation of terms, a consideration of the central findings of the public inquiry into the murder of the young black student Stephen Lawrence and looks at the possible impact of these findings on large organizations and institutions.

For a full and linked version of the report arising from the public inquiry into the death of Stephen Lawrence, visit:

☛ www.official-documents.co.uk/document/cm42/4262/sli-00.htm

London Lesbian and Gay Switchboard (LLGS)

London Lesbian and Gay Switchboard is a voluntary organization which aims to provide a 24-hour information, support and referral service for lesbians and gay men from all backgrounds throughout the United Kingdom.

London Lesbian and Gay Switchboard
PO Box 7324
London
N1 9QS

Tel: 020 7837 7324

☛ www.llgs.org.uk

National Disability Council (NDC)

The National Disability Council is an independent body with statutory duties to advise the Secretary of State for Education and Employment when asked to do so, or on its own initiative, on:

- the elimination of discrimination against disabled people;
- measures to reduce or eliminate such discrimination;
- the operation of the Disability Discrimination Act 1995 (DDA)

The NDC is charged with preparing:

- proposals for a code of practice on the rights of access to goods, facilities, services and premises;
- an annual report for Parliament at the end of each financial year.

The NDC works in close collaboration with the other equality bodies for Great Britain and Northern Ireland.

☛ www.disability-council.gov.uk

Positive action/discrimination

Positive *discrimination* is not allowed under the Race Relations and Sex Discrimination Acts. Positive *action* is. An example of unlawful positive discrimination would be if the Army declared that it wanted 25 per cent of its recruits to be black and recruited that proportion, while excluding equally qualified whites; that would be unlawful as it would have the effect of discriminating against white applicants on grounds of colour. Such action would normally be referred to as a 'quota system'. Although some countries have adopted this way of trying to redress imbalances in representation, quota systems tend to be inherently unfair and, some would say, more trouble than they are worth.

Positive action

There are two main areas in which positive action (as opposed to positive discrimination) may operate, where a particular minority ethnic group or sex is under represented:

1. Where there is under-representation, an employer may provide training solely for that group to help fit them for that work, or allow them to take advantage of training offered by other organizations (see **access courses**).
2. Employers may take positive steps – for instance, through advertising – to encourage applications from the under-represented group. For example, where there is shortfall of a particular ethnic group in an organization or one of its departments, measures can be taken to encourage and assist that specific group to apply for or qualify themselves for a job in order to make up such shortfalls.

A good real-world example of this is that of representation in London. The population of London is made up of large numbers of people from minority ethnic communities. Twenty-one of the London boroughs have 15 per cent or more of their populations made up from minority ethnic communities (Equal Opportunities Commission, 1993). At the end of 1992 only 2.17 per cent of serving police officers within the Metropolitan Police Service (which polices London) were from minority ethnic backgrounds (Commissioner of Police for the Metropolis, 1993).

It would be lawful, therefore, for the police service to take positive action through advertising which specifically encourages people from minority ethnic groups to apply to join, and they could also run courses designed to assist applicants to meet the entry requirements (see **access courses**). Although such courses are permitted by the legislation to be single race/colour, in fact, courses run by the Metropolitan Police Service have had both black and white participants.

The distinction between positive action/discrimination

We have already noted that while positive action is permitted under the legislation, positive discrimination is not. The debate about positive action seems to generate considerable emotion. The problem would seem to be the thin dividing line between action and discrimination. When the action is such that others feel they have been disadvantaged, someone will inevitably cry 'foul'.

One way of thinking about the difference between positive action and positive discrimination is to use the example of people running a 400-yard race on an athletics track. To ensure everyone has the same chance, ie an equal opportunity to compete, we would expect each person to start from the same point on the track. But, as we have discussed in detail throughout this book, there are sections of our society who, because they are in some way different from the majority, have to face prejudice and discrimination (at both personal and institutional level) and because of this they are placed at a disadvantage. To return to our example, such prejudice and discrimination has the effect of making members of those groups start the race from a point some way behind everyone else. To compete, they must then run faster and further.

Positive discrimination (which is *not* lawful), would close the race off to all except certain people, eg by taking on a candidate without advertising a vacancy or carrying out any selection processes, or placing particular people ahead of the 'starting line'.

Positive action, on the other hand (which *is* supported by the legislation) seeks only to bring everyone up to the same 'starting line' by allowing a narrow range of options such as access courses and targeted advertising. So positive action means that, for example, an employer can take action aimed at encouraging members of particular groups (sometimes called 'target groups'), who are under-represented within their company or organization, to apply for vacancies for work previously done exclusively or mainly by the opposite sex or by a particular ethnic group. At the time of writing this, for example, the National Health Service was advertising for nurses, and actively encouraging men to apply, as they are very under-represented in nursing. This is perfectly lawful.

Once people are able to start from the same 'starting line', however, they must then compete with others and be judged on their merits as individuals. The best person for the job or position should be selected, regardless of their gender, ethnicity or marital status.

 www.cre.gov.uk   www.eoc.org.uk

Public Order Act 1986

Whilst there is general freedom of speech in this country, legislators (people who make new laws) have considered that there are certain types of behaviour or speech which, if allowed, would stir up racial hatred against members of minority ethnic groups in our society. The Public Order Act 1986 defines as criminal offences the following ways of saying or doing things in public intended or likely to stir up racial hatred:

- use of words or behaviour;
- publishing or distributing written material;
- performing a play in public;
- distributing, showing or playing a recording;
- broadcasting over the radio or on television; and
- possessing racially inflammatory material.

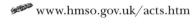 www.hmso.gov.uk/acts.htm

Race Relations Act 1976

Background to the legislation

Post-war immigration control had already begun in the late 1940s, at a time when there was great demand for labour and many industries were actively recruiting people from the West Indies. In fact, only a third of those entering for work were black, the rest being Irish, white Commonwealth and European. At this time, all Commonwealth citizens were able to enter Britain freely for work and settlement. Their status as 'British subjects' was confirmed by the British Nationality Act 1948.

During the 1950s, however, people began to argue that black 'immigrants' were placing a strain on housing, schools and social services. Some also claimed that black people were entering the UK so that they could live off the welfare state. Calls for immigration control began to be heard more frequently.

In 1958 there were serious public attacks on black people, primarily in Nottingham and Notting Hill, London, where a black man, Kelso Cochrane, was killed. Various surveys also began to reveal extensive prejudice and discrimination against black people. Sadly, in the eyes of many, racism had become respectable and the black population a problem.

There was pressure on the government of the day to tackle the situation, and it did so in two main ways. There was a succession of legislation aimed, on the one hand, at the control of immigration, and on the other, at promoting racial integration. The first Commonwealth Immigrants Act was introduced in 1962, requiring work vouchers to be issued for most British Commonwealth passport holders, ie those from countries with populations that were predominantly black. They couldn't enter without a voucher. This was despite the fact that there was still a shortage of skilled workers and little unemployment.

Further restrictions on the entry of Commonwealth immigrants were introduced in 1965 and 1968, and then in 1971 the right to permanent settlement was removed from new arrivals unless they were 'patrials', ie had a close connection with Britain by descent. The process culminated in the British Nationality Act 1981, which created three classes of citizenship:

1. British citizens upon whom there are no restrictions. This class of British citizenship is generally for those born in this country, or who had a parent, grandparent or spouse born here as a UK citizen, or have settled in this country for five years – these are mainly white.
2. British Dependent Territories citizens who, like those from Hong Kong, have a right to live in the colony to which they are connected – but no longer have a right of entry into the UK.
3. British overseas citizens, who are not members of Dependent Territories, and also do not have a right of entry to the UK.

While laws were passed controlling the number of people entering the country, a series of Acts were also passed from 1965 up to the most recent Race Relations Act of 1976, which promoted integration by making it illegal to discriminate under certain circumstances.

Race Relations Act 1976

Under the Race Relations Act 1976 it became unlawful to discriminate against someone on grounds of their colour, race, nationality or national or ethnic origins. The Act is enforced in two ways:

1. Enables a person discriminated against on racial grounds to go to a county court. If the alleged discrimination is in the field of employment, then they have redress at an industrial tribunal.
2. The **Commission for Racial Equality** was formed which, in certain circumstances, can assist those who feel they have been discriminated against. It can also carry out formal investigations into organizations where unlawful discrimination is suspected of being practised; in some circumstances without receiving a complaint.

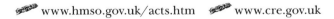 www.hmso.gov.uk/acts.htm   www.cre.gov.uk

Racial Equality Councils (RECs)

Racial equality councils are organizations that work in local areas, among local communities to promote racial equality and tackle racial discrimination. Some are funded by the Commission for Racial Equality. There are currently 108 RECs or similar organizations.

www.cre.gov.uk/about/recs.html

Examples of two local RECs:

Kingston racial equality council:

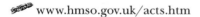 www.kingston.gov.uk/krec/Default.htm

Sheffield racial equality council:

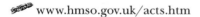 www.shef.ac.uk/uni/projects/oip/srec/

Rehabilitation of Offenders Act 1974

With the emphasis on sex and race discrimination that exists in this country it is all too easy to forget other legislation which, although not necessarily framed under the equal opportunities umbrella, nevertheless has the effect of promoting fairness for people. The Rehabilitation of Offenders Act is one such piece of legislation.

Its principal effect is to allow, in certain circumstances, the convictions of offenders to become 'spent'. This means that they do not have to be disclosed when applying for a job or for training, or when disclosing other previous convictions to a court. The type of conviction which may become spent and the time limits do vary both in terms of the offence and the sentence given to the offender. This legislation seeks to remove 'previous offence discrimination'.

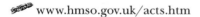 www.hmso.gov.uk/acts.htm

Royal Association for Disability and Rehabilitation (RADAR)

This is a national UK organization run by and working with disabled people which:

- campaigns for equal rights for disabled people;
- gives information and advice on all issues relating to disability;
- runs a national telephone helpline;
- promotes good practice and legislation which enables disabled people to live independently in the community;
- voices the wishes and concerns of disabled people;
- produces a wide range of publications and fact-packs on disability issues;
- supports around 500 member groups locally and nationally to help them become more effective in their work with disabled people.

Royal Association for Disability and Rehabilitation
25 Mortimer Street
London
W1N 8AB

 www.radar.org.uk/

Royal National Institute for the Blind (RNIB)

The RNIB provides help not only to totally blind people, but also to the 1½ million people in the UK with serious sight problems. It offers practical support and advice.

224–228 Great Portland Street
London
W1N 6AA

Call its helpline on 0345 66 99 99.

 www.rnib.org.uk

Royal National Institute for Deaf People (RNID)

RNID seeks to be a force for change with government, and public and private sector organizations. This includes changing attitudes towards people who are deaf or have hearing impairment and also to provide services to help improve their everyday lives. RNID also has a research interest in deafness.

Royal National Institute for Deaf People
105 Gower Street
London
WC1E 6AH

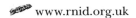 www.rnid.org.uk

Runnymede Trust

The Runnymede Trust is an independent research and policy agency which addresses itself specifically to the development of a successful multi-ethnic society. Its aim is to provide information, research and advice and to promote the value of diversity in our communities. Founded in 1968, the Trust is based in London, with the majority of its projects concentrated in England.

The Runnymede Trust
37a Grays Inn Road
London
WC1 8PS

www.fhit.org/runnymede/anniversa.html

Sex Discrimination Act 1975

Under the Sex Discrimination Act it is unlawful to discriminate on the grounds of sex or marital status in the areas of employment, trade union membership, education and the provision of goods and services, housing and advertising, except in certain circumstances. Discrimination can be against women or men, and also married people. Regarding employment, the Act applies from recruitment through what happens at work to dismissal. As with the Race Relations Act, the discrimination may be direct or indirect.

Sex discrimination which is lawful

Several sections of the Act allow different treatment of men and women in certain circumstances. These include:

* Special positive treatment of women because of pregnancy or childbirth.
* Where it is necessary to comply with earlier legislation. An example of both this and the previous provision is the case of a woman who was employed as a driver of a tanker carrying dangerous chemicals. It was discovered that the chemical was dangerous to women in pregnancy and in order to comply with the Health and Safety at Work Act she was transferred to other driving duties. She complained, but the industrial tribunal found that her employer was not guilty of unlawful discrimination on grounds of sex.
* Height requirements for the police and prison services. However, as noted already, the Metropolitan Police and other forces have foregone this provision as it tends to discriminate against certain ethnic groups.
* Employment as a minister of religion. Having said that, many readers will be aware of the public debate which took place in the Church of England in 1992/3 over the ordination of women priests.
* Employment as a midwife.
* To safeguard national security.
* Where the sex of a person is a genuine occupational qualification (see the section on GOQs above) because the job demands authentic gender characteristics.

www.hmso.gov.uk/acts.htm   www.eoc.org.uk

Stonewall

Stonewall is the national civil rights group working for legal equality and social justice for lesbians, gay men and bisexuals. It is a respected and effective campaigning organization working with a growing network of sympathetic politicians and alongside many grass roots groups.

Stonewall
16 Clerkenwell Close
London
EC1R 0AA
Tel: 020 7336 8860

 www.stonewall.org.uk

Trades Union Congress (TUC)

A selection of things the TUC does for its unions that relate to equal opportunities issues includes:

* bringing unions together to draw up common policies on issues like employment law, ways of tackling unemployment, and other workplace issues;
* pressing the Government to implement policies that will benefit people at work;
* campaigning on economic and social issues;
* carrying out research on employment-related issues.

23–28 Great Russell Street
London
WC1B 3LS

 www.tuc.org.uk/

Treaty of Rome 1957

In 1957 the Treaty of Rome established the European Community which was to provide for, among other things, the freedom of movement of the labour force and equality of opportunity. Article 119 of the treaty provides that men and women should receive equal pay for equal work.

> *Article 119* Each member state shall during the first stage ensure and subsequently maintain the application of the principle that men and women should receive equal pay for equal work.
>
> For the purpose of this Article, 'pay' means the ordinary basic or minimum wage or salary and any other consideration whether in cash or

in kind, which the worker receives, directly or indirectly, in respect of his employment from his employer.

Equal pay without discrimination based on sex, means:

(a) that pay for the same work at piece rates shall be calculated on the basis of the same unit of measurement;
(b) that pay for work at time rates shall be the same for the same job.

 www.europa.eu.int/index.htm

Universal Declaration of Human Rights

There is a tendency in some circles to view the emergence of thinking about equal opportunities as fashionable, even faddish. In fact, the basic principles of human rights which underpin the equal opportunities legislation of today are enshrined in the Universal Declaration of Human Rights, which was adopted by the General Assembly of the United Nations on 10 December 1948. Although many other treaties have since been made, the Universal Declaration still forms the foundation stone for them.

The whole declaration resounds with the issues we have been discussing in this book, but some selected articles illustrate its scope:

Article 1 All human beings are born free and equal in dignity and rights. They are endowed with reason and conscience and should act towards one another in a spirit of brotherhood.
Article 2 Everyone is entitled to all the rights and freedoms set forth in this declaration, without distinction of any kind, such as race, colour, sex, language, religion, political or other opinion, national or social origin, property, birth or other status.
Article 23(1) Everyone has the right to work, to free choice of employment, to just and favourable conditions of work, and to protection against unemployment.
Article 23(2) Everyone without any discrimination has the right to equal pay for equal work.

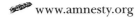 www.amnesty.org

Vicarious liability

In the case of issues relating to employment, responsibility for complying with the provisions of both the Sex Discrimination and Race Relations Acts generally rests with both the individual *and* the employer, providing the alleged misconduct arose in the course of the person's employment. If, for example, a personnel officer in a company were discriminating on grounds of sex or race in selection interviews, both the personnel officer and their employer would be liable. The employer would be said to be vicariously liable.

The employer might have a defence if it were proved that all reasonable steps had been taken to prevent the employee from discriminating. Such steps might include:

- an equal opportunities policy;
- equal opportunities training for each employee; and
- procedures for dealing with breaches of the EO policy or any breaches of the legislation.

In fact, the law goes even further by preventing the application of any type of pressure on any person or the giving of instructions or assistance to that person to discriminate against another. So a person in authority cannot instruct another to discriminate. An example of this would be an employer who issued instruction to an employment agency that they were not to send any black candidates for a particular job. Given the responsibility which rests on both the employer and employee, the need for equal opportunities policies become clearer.

 www.cre.gov.uk   www.eoc.org.uk

Victimization

There is a further offence under the Race Relations and Sex Discrimination Acts – that of victimization. This provision is designed to protect those who, in good faith, have made allegations about discrimination, started proceedings or given evidence in proceedings brought under the Acts. It is aimed at protecting a person who has made a complaint or brought a case (or assisted in one) under the legislation from being harassed, victimized or persecuted because of their complaint. Such victimization is often aimed at dissuading the person from pursuing their legitimate grievance and is a separate offence under the Acts.

An example of victimization would be where an employee institutes proceedings believing he has been passed over for promotion because he is black. A colleague gives evidence on his behalf and in the pay round the complainant and colleague are the only members of staff to be refused a pay rise. This would be a clear case of victimization under the Act (Malone, 1993).

www.hmso.gov.uk/acts.htm

References

Abercrombie, N *et al* (1994) *Dictionary of Sociology*, London: Penguin.

Allport, G W (1954) *The Nature of Prejudice*, New York: Addison Wesley.

Banton, M (1973) *Police Community Relations*, London: Collins.

Becker, H S (1963) Outsiders: Studies in the Sociology of Deviance, New York: Macmillan.

Calvert, S and Calvert, P (1992) *Sociology Today*, Hemel Hempstead: Harvester Wheatsheaf.

Chevigny, H (1962) *My Eyes have a Cold Nose*, New Haven, Conn: Yale University Press.

Collins, H (1992) *The Equal Opportunities Guide*, Oxford: Blackwell.

Commissioner of Police for the Metropolis (1993) Annual Report to the Home Secretary.

Davenport,W (1965) 'Sexual Patterns and their Regulations in a Society of the South West Pacific', in Beach, F (ed), *Sex and Behaviour*, New York: Wiley.

Equal Opportunities Commission (1986) *Guidelines for Equal Opportunities Employers*.

Equal Opportunities Commission (1993) *A Short Guide to the Equal Opportunities Commission*.

Equal Opportunities Commission (1993) *Women and Men in Britain 1993*.

Foot, H (1986) 'Humour and Laughter', in Hargie, O, *A Handbook of Communication Skills*, London: Routledge.

Giddens, A (1989) *Sociology*, Cambridge: Polity Press.

Goffman, E (1990) *Stigma: Notes on the Management of Spoiled Identity*, London: Penguin.

Hargie, O (1986) *A Handbook of Communication Skills*, London: Routledge.

Homans, H (1987) 'Man-made myth: the reality of being a woman scientist in the NHS', in Spencer, A and Podmore, D (eds), *In a Man's World: Essays on Women in Male Dominated Professions*, London: Tavistock.

Jowell, R *et al.* (eds) (1992) *British Social Attitudes, 9th Report*, Aldershot: Dartmouth Publishing.

Macpherson, W (1999) *The Macpherson Report*, London: The Stationery Office.

Malone, M (1993) *Discrimination Law*, London: Kogan Page.

Money, J and Ehrdhardt, A A (1972) *Man and Woman/Boy and Girl*, Baltimore: Johns Hopkins University Press.

Poulter, S M (1986) *English Law and Ethnic Minority Customs*, London: Butterworths.

Segal, L (1990) *Slow Motion: Changing Masculinities Changing Men*, London: Virago.

Shepherd, G (1987) 'Rank, Gender and Homosexuality: Mombasa as a key to understanding sexual options', in Caplan, P (ed), *The Social Construction of Sexuality*, London: Tavistock.

Spinks, T & Clements, P (1993) *A Practical Guide to Facilitation Skills: A Real World Approach*, London: Kogan Page.

Vallely, P (1993) 'Driving home the message on sex discrimination', *Police*, September 1993.

Walvin, J (1984) *Passage to Britain: Immigration in British history and politics, a series of TV documentaries on Channel Four*, London: Pelican.

Index